Resources in Education

# Teaching Science in the Primary School

## Book Two:
### Action Planning for Effective Science Teaching

## Edited by
## Alan Cross and Gill Peet

Northcote House

ISBN 0-7463-0684-9

**British Library Cataloguing-in-Publication Data**
A catalogue record for this book is available
from the British Library

© 1998 by Alan Cross & Gill Peet on behalf of all contributors

First published in 1998 by Northcote House Publishers Ltd,
Plymbridge House, Estover Road, Plymouth PL6 7PY, United Kingdom.
Tel: Plymouth (01752) 202368. Fax: (01752) 202330.

Typeset by Kestrel Data, Exeter.
Printed and bound in Great Britain.

# Contents

*Notes on Contributors*                                                  vii

1  Introduction: Taking Action for Science                                 1
   *Alan Cross and Gill Peet*

2  Children's Learning in Science                                          8
   *Alan Cross and Gill Peet*

3  Spreading the Message: Exploring Language
     and Learning in Science                                              23
   *David Heywood*

4  Progression and Differentiation in Science:
     Some General Strategies                                              34
   *Stuart Naylor and Brenda Keogh*

5  Progression and Differentiation in Science:
     Some Specific Strategies                                             44
   *Stuart Naylor and Brenda Keogh*

6  Equal Opportunities                                                    59
   *Gill Peet*

7  Science in the Early Years                                             75
   *Karen Hartley and Christine Macro*

8  Process Skills in Primary Science                                      97
   *David Byrne*

9 Implementing Assessment and Recording as
   a Constructive Process                                116
   *Ron Ritchie*

10 Information and Communication Technology
   (ICT) in Primary Science                              130
   *Alan Cross and Tony Birch*

11 Cross-Curricular Links in Science                     154
   *Carole Naylor and Anthony Pickford*

12 Home–School Links                                     168
   *Alan Cross and Conrad Chapman*

13 The Role of the Science Co-ordinator                  183
   *Gill Peet*

14 Monitoring and Evaluation                             194
   *Alan Cross and Alan Chin*

*Index*                                                  208

# Notes on Contributors

## EDITORS

### Alan Cross

Alan has taught both infants and juniors as a class teacher and deputy headteacher. Later he led Salford LEA's Primary Science and Technology Unit for three years. Presently he is Lecturer in Primary Education at the Department of Education, University of Manchester. He now leads both the science and the design and technology elements on the one-year PGCE primary course. He runs short courses for primary teachers, leads development and evaluation projects, has addressed a number of overseas international conferences and is an Ofsted-trained Inspector. He has written widely in the areas of science, design and technology and information technology including *Design and Technology 5–11* published by Hodder and Stoughton (1994) and *Coordinating design and technology across the primary school* published by Falmer Press (1998). Currently Alan is researching teaching styles in the primary classroom.

### Gill Peet

Gill is an experienced class teacher of both infants and juniors and taught for a number of years in a multi-racial primary school. She worked formerly as an advisory teacher for primary science and technology before becoming a senior lecturer at Manchester Metropolitan University where she was responsible for co-ordinating the science in education course for B.Ed students. She also teaches design and technology. Gill has led many INSET sessions, including 20-day science courses. She has recently conducted research into children's investigations in science and has published in the area of equal opportunities. She is an Ofsted-trained Inspector.

## BACKGROUND OF WRITERS

### Tony Birch

Tony is a General Adviser with Bolton LEA and has specific responsibility for primary information technology. He has experience as a primary school IT co-ordinator, trainer with Manchester LEA and co-director of two Manchester University IT projects. Tony is an Ofsted-trained Inspector and has experience as a deputy head in two primary schools.

### David Byrne

David acts as a consultant to LEAs and schools and is an Ofsted-trained Inspector. He has published widely, including materials for Lego Dacta, five titles for the Longmans Book Project, the BP science-based resource, *Living with Traffic*, and the Teacher Time-savers Publication *Physical Processes*. David is a regular contributor to both *Junior* and *Child Education* magazines. He has had over 25 years experience in primary education in both Britain and abroad. He has taught across the 5–11 range and has held posts of responsibility for science in two large urban primary schools. In 1985 he took up the post of Teacher Adviser where he co-ordinated a team of advisory teachers supporting primary schools in science and technology in Bury LEA. This involved the delivery of a range of courses both regionally and nationally. In 1992 he took up the post of Course Leader of the Science B.Ed (Hons) Department at the North East Wales Institute of Higher Education. David works as a freelance educational writer, inspector and consultant.

### Conrad Chapman

Conrad is the head of a multi-cultural, multi-racial community school in Oldham (Greenhill Community School). He was the first co-ordinator of the Royal Society of Arts (RSA) Home–School Contract of Partnership Project and is currently a part-time INSET provider and lecturer at Manchester University's School of Education. His more recent publications in the home–school sphere include *Home–School Work in Britain* and *A Willing Partnership*.

### Alan Chin

Alan is an experienced primary school teacher and is currently deputy headteacher of Ludworth Primary School in Stockport where he has specific responsibility for science and whole-school curriculum development. In the areas of science education, Alan has given support to initial teacher training students at both Manchester University and Manchester Metropolitan University. He has also been involved in providing INSET to serving teachers, on the role of the science co-ordinator in the inspection process, and to deputy head-teachers on aspects of management. Alan has worked with the Manchester Museum of Science and Industry in the development of support materials for their exhibits.

### Karen Hartley

Karen has had many years experience as a teacher of young children. Before becoming an advisory teacher for science she was deputy headteacher of a primary school with responsibility for the infant department. Whilst working as an advisory teacher she was involved in the SPACE research undertaken by CRIPSAT at Liverpool University. She is an endorsed trainer of the High Scope approach to the development of young children's learning and is co-author of teaching materials for primary science. She is presently employed as a senior lecturer at Edge Hill University College where she teaches on the BA and BSc courses and is an INSET provider on both award-bearing and short courses.

### David Heywood

David is a senior lecturer in the Department of Sciences Education at the Manchester Metropolitan University. He works on initial teacher training courses and co-ordinates the primary INSET programme including GEST-funded 10- and 20-day science courses for primary teachers. He has worked in several primary schools as a co-ordinator for both science and technology. His current research interest is in the field of language and interpretation of scientific ideas. A former advisory teacher in science and technology, he has experience of working in both primary schools and secondary schools. Prior to his present position, David was deputy headteacher of a large primary school.

### Brenda Keogh

Brenda is currently senior lecturer at Manchester Metropolitan University where she is involved in initial and in-service education. Presently Brenda directs Streamwatch UK, a national environmental project. Prior to this, she taught mainly in primary schools and worked as an advisory teacher and National Curriculum Co-ordinator. She is involved in the work of the Association for Science Education and the British Association. Her professional interests are mostly shared with her husband Stuart Naylor, and include teacher professional development, public access to science and the connection between teaching and learning. Her most recent publication is *Starting Points for Science*, which outlines an innovative approach to learning science through concept cartoons, which are currently being used in the 'Science on the Underground' project.

### Chris Macro
Chris taught for many years in primary schools and for five years led the Primary Science and Technology initiative in St Helens LEA. She was for a time a member of CRIPSAT at the University of Liverpool and was co-author of teacher training materials for science education. Chris has had a number of short articles published and is presently conducting research into the use of information technology in science education. She works at Edge Hill University College where, as senior lecturer, she teaches in the Primary Science department. Chris provides INSET on both short and award-bearing courses and acts as an educational consultant.

### Carole Naylor
Carole worked as a class teacher in primary schools for a number of years before joining Manchester LEA's team for primary science and technology. Since 1988 she has worked at University College, Chester where as a senior lecturer and section leader for Science she teaches on courses of initial teacher education and the PGCE (Primary) programme.

### Stuart Naylor
Stuart is currently principal lecturer at Manchester Metropolitan University where he is involved in initial and in-service teacher education. Prior to this he taught mainly in secondary schools in this country and the USA and worked as an advisory teacher. He is involved in the work of the Association for Science Education and the British Association. His professional interests are mostly shared with his wife Brenda Keogh, and include teacher professional development, public access to science and the connection between teaching and learning. His most recent publication is *Starting Points for Science*, which outlines an innovative approach to learning science through concept cartoons, which are currently being used in the 'Science on the Underground' project.

### Tony Pickford
After sixteen years as a primary class teacher in Tameside, Tony moved to University College Chester in 1990 to teach on the B.Ed

and PGCE (Primary) programmes. He now teaches in both the technology and teacher education departments on a range of modules. Tony has published articles in several journals, including *Primary Science Review* and the *British Journal of Educational Technology*. Tony is also ICT co-ordinator for the School of Education.

**Ron Ritchie**
Ron is Head of the Department for Professional Development at Bath Spa University College and teaches on initial and in-service education programmes. Ron has taught in primary and secondary schools and was an advisory teacher for primary science in Avon. He is author of books and articles on the teaching of science and technology including *Primary Science: Making it Work* (with Chris Ollerenshaw) (1997), and *Primary Design and Technology: a Process for Learning* (1995) both published by David Fulton. He has been involved in several research projects in science, one of which focused on assessment and was funded by the National Primary Centre.

# 1
# Introduction:
# Taking Action for Science

## *Alan Cross and Gill Peet*

## INTRODUCTION

This book builds upon the advice set out by the authors in *Teaching Science in the Primary School: Book 1*, which looked at the context, challenges and suggested strategies relating to the subjects of each chapter. In Book 2 each chapter from Book 1 is developed in specific, practical steps. These can be employed by individual teachers or groups of teachers to improve science taught in the primary years. Authors have not attempted to do everything for the reader, rather they have sought to provide a strong line for development which it is hoped when combined with other chapters will give teachers many options and areas to develop.

Both books are intended to be readable and practical, addressing issues which primary teachers and students in training will encounter as they seek to implement and develop science as part of the primary curriculum. The authors have written to a general teaching audience so that non-specialists will be able to use the book as well as those with a science background. It is expected that school science co-ordinators and primary teacher trainers might use selected activities with colleagues and students. To this end the authors have generally taken strong themes from their writing in Book 1 and devised activities which help primary teachers to build from where they are now.

Throughout, the authors recognise the need for the developments described to be implemented across the whole school so that the impact of changes will have greatest effect. They have, however, in each case provided for one stated aim of the books, that is that

1

individual teachers can utilise the books to develop their own practice.

Activities in this book are often sequential. Authors have suggested an order in which activities be tackled, although readers may wish to vary this. An activity may be particularly relevant to your development and so may be given more emphasis. The writers have attempted in many cases to give readers guidance about the time which might be required for activities. These suggestions are only for guidance, and we cannot hope that this advice will be correct for all readers. However, we would suggest that you set yourself a time limit and try to stick to it. This is good preparation for classroom implementation of these ideas as time will always be a constraint.

In editing the book we have been very aware that science is only one of eleven subjects for primary teachers. The books can be used in two ways. They can be read from cover to cover. This will give an overall picture of science development opportunities. Some readers, however, will select particular themes and read the companion chapters from Books 1 and 2 together. When you are using sections of Book 2 we would encourage you to **re-read the relevant chapter in Book 1** as the chapters have been written with this in mind.

> *Note*: References to Book 1 will give the book number, the name(s) of the author)s), and the chapter number, e.g. '(Bk. 1, Cross and Peet, 1)'.

Book 2 does not emphasise the three sections which were the basis of Book 1, nor were authors asked to deal in each chapter with context, challenges and strategies as they were in Book 1. However, we have maintained the order of chapters so that cross-referencing between the two books is made easier. The flexibility given to the authors has, we feel, resulted in a range of styles which have been selected to suit the subjects. Authors have once again, as in Book 1, kept their attention firmly on children's science, the classrooms in which it takes place and the teaching which leads directly to learning.

We would suggest that you keep an informal diary or establish a file as a focus for your professional development. The construction of a simple action plan for science in your classroom or school will be a useful strategy for you (see Figure 1.1). Be prepared to ask lots of professional questions about science education in a similar way to the questions we want children to ask about science. Your professional questions about science may be addressed to yourself:

- do I have enough background knowledge?

- how can I make more of my time with children engaged in science?

or to others (including colleagues, consultants, books, course presenters, LEA representatives):

- how can I support my electricity topic with a local visit?

- how can I promote ICT through science?

---

**Possible areas of concern**

**Areas identified**

**Prioritise these:**

| Long term | Short term |
|---|---|
| | |

**Action to be taken**
**Deadlines**

**Review/evaluation**

---

Fig. 1.1. Constructing an action plan

## SCIENTIFIC QUESTIONING

In Book 1 we emphasised a number of things in the introductory chapter, one of which was that what humans understand in science is provisional. Meteorologists studying thunderstorms know a lot about lightning but still cannot explain why it chooses one place to come to ground and not another, or why it is that during a big thunderstorm huge 'sprites' occur. These bright illuminations which extend up, high above the storm clouds, were recently discovered by astronauts and high-flying test pilots. Scientists as yet have little idea what 'sprites' are. Many theories may come and go alongside observations and investigations before we find answers, if we ever do!

3

The provisional nature of scientific theory is a fact and is a great strength in science. It means that we can learn from new observations. However, it does mean that scientists will appear to get things 'wrong', that is, propose and use theories which subsequently prove to be incorrect. The desire to refine and amend ideas is at the heart of science and as such we ought to encourage this in ourselves and in our children.

Thus we find that scientific questioning is at the heart of the subject: children and teachers need the confidence to ask questions. Perhaps the most significant question to teachers of science in the primary years is, 'how does this child understand this scientific concept?' The 'constructivist' approach accepts that children have 'alternative understandings' about scientific concepts. Teachers are encouraged to make the elicitation of ideas from children the basis for future challenges which allow children to re-examine ideas.

## OUTLINE OF THE CHAPTERS

In Chapter 2 Cross and Peet challenge readers to examine their scientific ideas about everyday phenomena. This elicitation of ideas is at the heart of the constructivist approach. They then switch the attention of the reader to children in school. They finally ask that teachers consider ways to incorporate such elicitation and challenge in their planning. These approaches avoid the need for a book like this to mention every scientific concept. Teachers understand the need for simple yet effective approaches in the classroom.

Chapter 3 re-emphasises the importance of language in children's learning of science. Examples and approaches are provided which ask that the reader considers words that we use and the variety of meaning which can prove a challenge to teachers. Heywood shows how agreement should be sought and that we will be witnessing an evolution in the understanding of ideas. The emphasis is on interpretation which is an honest admission that teachers themselves often have very different perceptions within science concepts from their children.

Keogh and Naylor provide readers with practical and realistic approaches to the related areas of progression and differentiation in science. Their approach here is to emphasise the importance of a whole-school approach. Thus Chapter 4 deals with general strategies and is followed in Chapter 5 by activities dealing with specific strategies. Their framework which was introduced in Book 1 is now used to focus the attention of the reader. They recognise that teachers ought to prepare for the stage above that which they expect children

4

to achieve. Thus the teacher is in a good position to respond to children who attain well and to other attainment groups. These chapters are without doubt pertinent to the whole of primary education but have been written carefully with science in mind.

In Chapter 6 on equal opportunities, Peet may be felt to be preaching to the converted. With this in mind, she has chosen to focus on the necessity to influence colleagues. She tackles the issue of prejudice head on, building upon the foundation of her earlier contribution (Bk. 1, Peet, 6).

A chapter which should be considered carefully by all readers is Chapter 7 on science in the early years by Macro and Hartley. They offer a range of activities which build importantly on their identified need for all teachers to build up their scientific understanding. This can easily be overlooked as an issue at Key Stage 1 as it is perceived to be a serious problem only at Key Stage 2. Hartley and Macro use a range of media to assist your consideration of important areas like play, collaboration and planning.

Byrne encourages an active approach in Chapter 8 to the promotion of the science process. He emphasises the need for children to progress in the area of science process capability. To this end he asks the reader to trial and evaluate approaches to planning science, developing strands within science process and children's process planning.

Ritchie recognises the importance of assessment and record-keeping in primary science. He advocates a broadly constructivist approach which complements the other writing in the book. His practical strategies will give teachers a range of sound alternatives, and after trying them out most teachers will be in a much stronger position to say which forms of assessment suit which situations. His approach is practical, recognising that primary teachers lack the time to assess nine subjects. He does, however, offer practical and useful ideas which can be used to supply information back into the teaching and planning cycle which is so much part of teaching.

The present place of IT in science in primary education is the starting point for Cross and Birch in Chapter 10. They provide for an audit and an examination of what children are actually doing on the computer in science. A suggested framework is given which is realistic and achievable. They recognise that there is a dearth of resource-based software (software with a scientific content) of quality. They also suggest that access to computers will have to change significantly to allow the sort of science work which has been demonstrated as possible. There is an emphasis on progression which might culminate in an examination of IT in science across the school.

5

Technology in a quite different form and in an historical context forms the second part of Chapter 11. Naylor and Pickford demonstrate the power of a carefully selected context for stimulating genuine investigation across a number of subjects including science. This is preceded by an examination of National Curriculum objectives for different subjects and the relation of science to the whole curriculum.

Chapter 12 builds on the excellent advice given by Chapman in Book 1. Here Cross and Chapman provide a number of activities which should provide starting points for parental involvement in science. For most primary schools parental involvement is not a new thing. There appears to be little doubt about its positive effects. For those promoting science, parents can be valuable allies in every respect.

If primary schools are going to address any of the issues mentioned in this book, a school co-ordinator or subject manager will have to be involved. This person will require considerable skill as well as considerable personal reserves! This area is tackled by Peet in Chapter 13. The personal qualities she encourages co-ordinators to develop will mean that they can begin to address all the issues and implement the ideas she put forward in Book 1 (Bk. 1, Peet, 13).

Co-ordinators of science in primary schools are almost certain to be seen as having a role in monitoring the subject. This is a recent and substantial change in the perception of the role of the subject co-ordinator, which may be why the term 'subject manager' has grown in popularity. Cross and Chin provide a range of activities in Chapter 14 building on their earlier work in Chapter 14 in Book 1. Here co-ordinators will see opportunities to audit, to examine work in the classroom and to come to a view of how the children and therefore the school is performing.

## CONCLUSION

Primary teachers face a considerable challenge as we move into the early years of the twenty-first century. Society will expect more and more from a system of primary education which was developed in the late nineteenth century! The generalist class-teacher system of primary education may not be the best way to deliver primary education. However, within current and likely future spending constraints it is hard to envisage changes which will materially change the situation. The anomaly in funding between Year 6 and Year 7 remains as a reminder to all of us that different values are placed by some people on education in different educational phases. This line of argument may be a dead end owing to spending restrictions and a lack of will to tackle it. Primary schools must make the most of what they have. Science is now compulsory, and we have an incredible track record as we have moved from little primary science in the 1970s to universal primary science in the 1990s. Whilst that momentum may be impossible to maintain, we must continue to work at improving children's primary science. This means the very best management of science with one objective in mind, that is, the children's attainment.

# 2
# Children's Learning in Science

*Alan Cross and Gill Peet*

## INTRODUCTION

This chapter follows on from its companion chapter in Book 1 (Bk. 1, McGuigan and Schilling, 2) which describes research and experience in the important area of children's learning in science. McGuigan and Schilling provide practical advice so that primary teachers might account for children's ideas in their teaching of science.

The activities that follow can be used by you in your own classroom or might be used by a group of teachers wishing to explore children's learning in science. The aim of the activities is to assist teachers in exploring their personal ideas about scientific principles, followed by consideration of children's understanding. It is then suggested that you account for this exploration of ideas in plans for teaching. The first activity asks for a general overview of children's ideas in the classroom.

## THE IMPORTANCE OF CHILDREN'S IDEAS

In our experience, teachers often have some difficulty appreciating why it is so important to consider and account for children's ideas about scientific concepts. We wish to illustrate this below by referring briefly to work done by Joseph Nussbaum (1985). There are few issues in science so important to primary teachers as the ways in which children learn scientific concepts. Without such consideration it is possible that teachers will find themselves using a new language (scientific terminology) with young children and speaking at cross purposes with the children. It is therefore important that you elicit both their understanding and your own.

8

Nussbaum asked children about the force of gravity. He recogni. that most people start with an egocentric view of the world. Your children see only evidence of a 'flat' Earth. They fail to recognise evidence of a round Earth. He saw three concepts as crucial to a move towards the scientific view of a spherical Earth (see Figure 2.1).

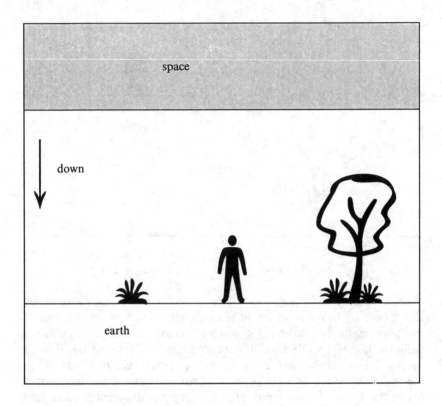

Figure 2.1. Three essential concepts in formation of a scientific world view (from Nussbaum, 1985)

He found that many young children could recall the fact that the Earth is a sphere. However, many of these children retained strong elements of their earlier 'flat' Earth view. Some have a world view something like (b) rather than (a) in Figure 2.2. This may be a consequence of experiencing a 'flat' environment. Observation, therefore, appears to be at odds with what they have been told about a spherical Earth. Some children therefore appear to adapt rather than change their original view of a flat Earth.

9

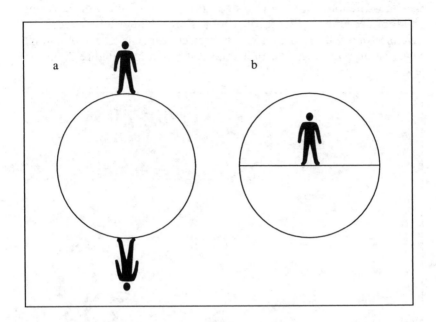

Figure 2.2. Alternative world views (from Nussbaum, 1985)

Nassbaum goes on to describe numerous other models or views of the Earth held by those children he worked with. Thus we can see that a teacher might be misled by a child using scientific vocabulary (spherical, orbit) while retaining an intermediate view of the Earth's shape. A teacher discussing the changing appearance of the moon in the night sky (i.e. our view of the illuminated side of the moon as it orbits the Earth) with a child, might be continually frustrated to find the child cannot fit this idea into their model of the Earth. Related examples are given by Heywood in the companion volume (Bk. 1, Heywood, 3).

Another area of research reveals something of the development of ideas in children. Osborne and Freyburg (1985) looked at the understanding of the concept 'animal' in different age groups of children. They found that, for example, when asked about an earthworm, 50 per cent of 5- and 6-year-old children said that an earthworm was an animal. The proportion of older teenagers who agreed with this was even higher (70 per cent). However, they found that a large proportion (60 per cent) of 13-year-olds said that the earthworm was not an animal. Thus, a dip in understanding was revealed around the end of primary and at the beginning of secondary education. This dip appeared throughout their data and has been replicated in similar studies around the world. Explanations of this include the increasing maturity of the children, the children's appreciation of the complexity of the world and even that children begin to expect 'hard' questions from teachers. Similar studies with teachers (Summers and Kruger, 1990; Smith and Peacock, 1990) reveal a significant range in understanding of even basic scientific concepts.

These studies tell us that scientific concepts might rarely be accepted and understood in single lessons. They also suggest that didactic teaching alone is unlikely to be fully effective with all children. Harlen (1992) provides a straightforward explanation for this in terms of children adapting existing ideas and clinging on to them. Harlen describes children who are very reluctant to let go of familiar and yet unscientific ideas. Harlen points out that as these children develop the ability to carry out fair, scientific tests they will be in a better position to refute incorrect ideas.

Children do not appear to be empty vessels to be filled, and so as teachers we need to be sophisticated in our approach. We would say that the basis of that sophistication is a recognition of the importance and range of children's alternative understandings and that constructivist approaches to teaching offer the best approach to this complexity.

All of this should be reassuring to the teachers who have found that children don't always respond as you might expect to even the best prepared lessons. It is not necessarily your fault! Science learning is not a simple matter! This is one reason why in this chapter we will ask you to consider some of your own ideas about some basic principles in science before you focus your attention on the children's understanding.

McGuigan and Schilling (Bk. 1, McGuigan and Schilling, 2) describe strategies to promote conceptual change in children's ideas. The first step is the elicitation of children's ideas through dialogue based on open questioning or through drawings where children use pictures to represent their understanding. Once teachers have an accurate idea of the child's understanding, McGuigan and Schilling suggest approaches to further support learning that include:

- helping children to test their ideas through investigation;

- encouraging generalisations of instances of the concept from one context to another;

- extending the range of evidence available;

- exploring the use of children's vocabulary through discussion.

These are introduced in the later activities.

### Activity 1 – Children's ideas in your classroom
(Time required: 40 minutes)
Use the prompts in Figure 2.3 to consider how children's ideas about science manifest themselves in the classroom and consider the sort of messages we give to them about their ideas.

| | |
|---|---|
| When do these appear?<br> in discussion?<br> during classtime?<br> on the playground?<br> at home?<br> at play? | How do we react to children's ideas?<br> do we value them?<br> can we integrate them into<br>  class science?<br> how do we react to alternative<br>  ideas? |
| | Children's ideas in science |
| Does the room encourage children's ideas?<br>displays?     books?<br>posters?     organisation?<br>time to talk about science? | How can we move children's ideas towards a scientific view?<br>– questions<br>– challenges<br>– new evidence<br>– generalisations |

Figure 2.3. Considering children's ideas in the classroom

### Activity 2 – Putting the bang into science!
(Time required: 20 minutes)
Here we'd like you to practise re-examining your own ideas. By this

we do not want you to assume that you are wrong. You will have a fairly accurate scientific view about many things. However, like many adults you may explain phenomena in 'everyday' language.

Try this: imagine you are blowing up a balloon. You fill it. Predict what will happen if you keep blowing. You keep blowing. The balloon bursts. Why did it burst? You might like to use the proforma in Figure 2.4.

| In science we are looking at............................................ | | |
|---|---|---|
| In my life I have seen this when... | I noticed that... | I think that this is so because... |
| The key word/s is/are... | | I want to see if I am right so I will... |
| The result is that... | | Can I now make a generalisation? |

Figure 2.4. Examining my own ideas about a scientific concept

In your explanation do you talk about too much air? About pressure? About the size of the balloon?

If you used 'everyday' vocabulary this does not mean that you don't have a scientific understanding. If you can blow balloons up without overfilling them then you must have some understanding!

Your explanation might include such words and phrases as 'extra air in', 'pushing', 'pressing' or 'forcing'. If you have used the word 'pressure' you may be very close to a scientific view which would talk about pressurised air in the balloon exerting a force on the inside of the balloon which pushes the balloon out. When pressure is increased further, the force is increased and gets closer to a point where the

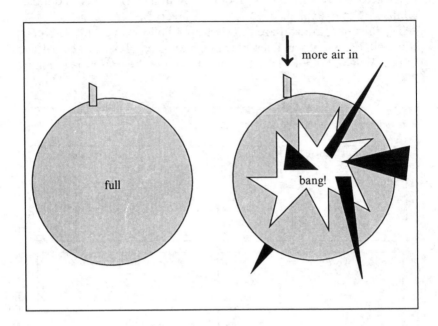

Figure 2.5. A balloon bursts

material used to make the balloon can no longer stand the force. Thus further increased pressure results in a catastrophic destruction of the balloon! The sudden, outward rush of the pressurised air produces the bang. The event is described as popping or bursting the balloon. (Take great care if you decide to demonstrate this event!)

## Activity 3 – Syphons on the go!
(Time required: 30 mins)
Firstly we suggest that you practically set up and operate a syphon (see Figure 2.6). You will need a safe place to work, a box, a plastic tube, two vessels and water.

Remember that you start water flowing through a syphon by immersing the plastic tube until it is entirely full of water. Put your fingers over the ends, lift the tube and place one end in the higher tank (full) and the other one in the lower (empty) and then release your fingers!

You should now have water running through the tube from the

higher to the lower vessel. Observe carefully. What happens? Particularly as the higher tank empties? Can you explain how and why this happens?

Try repeating it and while it is running try carefully lifting the tube in the upper vessel, very carefully so that you introduce a few bubbles. Watch the stream of bubbles. What happens if you let too much air in?

Try using our proforma from Figure 2.4. Have you ever heard of this happening in the real world? Can you draw a picture and explain what is happening? Could you change the demonstration to reveal more? In this way you would begin to experiment. Are there any questions you could ask which if answered would tell you more?

Could you change the difference in height between the vessels? The diameter of the tube? Predict what effect these changes will make. Try putting your finger over the bottom end of the tube while it is running. What happens? Now predict what will happen if you repeat this at the other end of the tube. Now try it.

Explanations offered in the past have included: 'it's downhill, it has got to go down!', 'Once it has started it just goes on'. So why does it

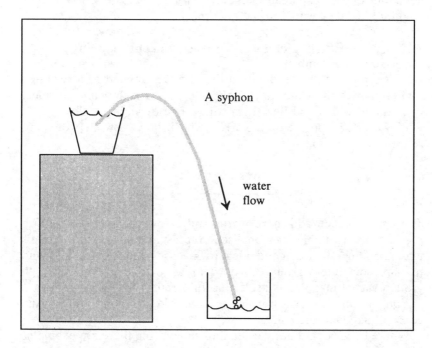

Figure 2.6. A syphon

15

not start on its own? Why can an air bubble stop it? (Further explanation is provided in the note at the end of this chapter.)

**Activity 4 – Eliciting children's ideas: annotated drawings**
(Time required: 1 hour)
In Book 1 McGuigan and Schilling give a number of options for eliciting children's scientific ideas. Later in this book Naylor and Keogh suggest other ideas including use of cartoons (see Chapter 5). Here we suggest that you begin with annotated drawings.

Ask the children to do a drawing or drawings to show how a phenomenon occurs. For example:

● In a topic or activity on sound you might ask: how is it that we hear things with our ears?

● In a topic or activity on forces, ask them to show why it is that a ball bounces.

By talking to the child about the picture afterwards you can get a good idea of their explanation. At this stage the child or you as teacher might add further words to the picture.

**Activity 5 – Eliciting children's ideas: concept mapping**
(Time required: 1 hour)
Here we present the child with a list of words related to a scientific topic of which the child may know. We then ask the child to select two related words and link them with a line or an arrow. They then write words or a phrase on the arrow which shows how the words are related. For example:

gives energy to
sun ————————▶ leaf

The children then add more words and arrows as they see fit. The product is a highly personalised representation of the child's understanding. It is a good idea to give some examples first and perhaps complete a group concept map as a training exercise. Such group concept mapping is itself a useful strategy for eliciting ideas.

You will find it very rewarding in terms of elicitation to discuss the concept map with the child.

Where children are not yet reading and writing there are examples of teachers using pictures that the children arrange in relation to one another and with arrows. Discussion can then follow about the relationships.

## IS THAT CORRECT?

This is the question scientists have to learn to ask, since much scientific understanding varies from the directly observable (young children have been surprised that the setting sun does not actually drop into the sea!). It is important that we as teachers learn to ask this question of the children's understanding. As you build a picture of the children's understanding, can you see ways of moving them towards a scientific view? Look back at results from the two previous activities for evidence of children's ideas.

| The children's understanding is . . . | Can be challenged by . . . |
| --- | --- |

- Could you change the materials they are dealing with?
- Can a new experience give them the opportunity to review their ideas?
- Would a test or experiment assist them?

We now turn to the suggestions made by McGuigan and Schilling in Book 1.

### Activity 6 – Challenging alternative ideas: extending the evidence base
(Time required: 30 minutes)
Do the children need to see more examples; for example, a wider range of floating objects including hollow and solid examples? Would a greater range of materials help; for example, a metal that is non-magnetic? Would the same test repeated 10, 20, 100 times always give the same result? Is the child looking at all the evidence?

| The children's understanding is . . . | We can look at other evidence including . . . |
| --- | --- |

## Activity 7 – Challenging alternative ideas: generalisations and predictions

(Time required: 30 minutes)

Can we make a generalisation to another context? For example, warmth and light improve the growth of seedlings in our classroom —is it true in the case of another plant?

Would our observation be repeated in other instances?

Is there a pattern in the data? Can we extrapolate? For example, the height of the average child increases with age, will this pattern continue indefinitely?

Can we test our generalisations?

| The children's understanding is . . . | Can we make a generalisation? |
|---|---|

## Activity 9 – Looking at your teaching plans

(Time required: 2 hours)

Now we suggest that you turn your attention to an area you are going to teach in science. We have given an example of this approach in Figure 2.8 where we use the same format as in Figure 2.7. Firstly you need to establish the broad area. Which scientific topic will you be dealing with? State the scientific concepts in terms of learning outcomes or learning objectives.

You may need to deal with concepts in turn. Think about the order you will deal with them. There is rarely an obvious order. You will want to deal first with simple examples that the child can relate to.

How will you approach these concepts practically? What practical investigations might the children make to answer a question? How will you determine the questions? A straightforward way to do this is to give the children time to observe a phenomenon and to generate questions. Another is to give them a challenge.

Now examine the concepts as you did the concepts in the early activities in this chapter. What is your understanding of . . . ? The aim here is to inform you and to deepen your understanding. You may also get a feel for the complexity of the concepts.

You might like to compare this with findings in a research paper. The bibliography and further reading section below list a selection of publications and topics.

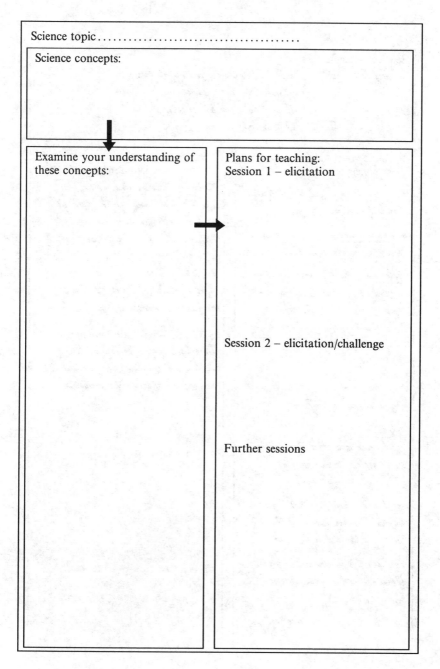

Figure 2.7. Building constructivism into our teaching plans

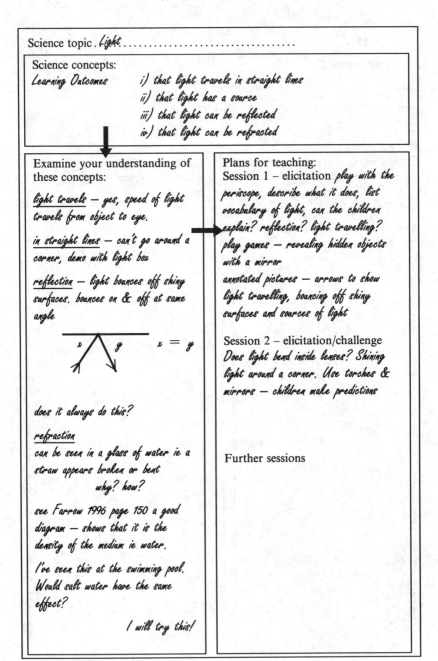

Science topic . *Light* . . . . . . . . . . . . . . . . . . . . . . . . . . . . . . .

Science concepts:

*Learning Outcomes*      *i) that light travels in straight lines*

*ii) that light has a source*

*iii) that light can be reflected*

*iv) that light can be refracted*

---

Examine your understanding of these concepts:

*light travels — yes, speed of light travels from object to eye.*

*in straight lines — can't go around a corner, demo with light box*

*reflection — light bounces off shiny surfaces. bounces on & off at same angle*

$$x = y$$

*does it always do this?*

*refraction*
*can be seen in a glass of water ie a straw appears broken or bent*
         *why? how?*

*see Farrow 1996 page 150 a good diagram — shows that it is the density of the medium ie water.*

*I've seen this at the swimming pool. Would salt water have the same effect?*

         *I will try this!*

Plans for teaching:
Session 1 – elicitation *play with the periscope, describe what it does, list vocabulary of light, can the children explain? reflection? light travelling? play games — revealing hidden objects with a mirror*

*annotated pictures — arrows to show light travelling, bouncing off shiny surfaces and sources of light*

Session 2 – elicitation/challenge
*Does light bend inside lenses? Shining light around a corner. Use torches & mirrors — children make predictions*

Further sessions

Figure 2.8. An example of developing science concepts

20

# CONCLUSION

Following a constructivist approach to the teaching of science will give you a sound foundation for furthering the children's achievement in all aspects of science. It will provide you with information about the particular children you have and questions about learning which are likely to appear and reappear. You will find that assessment in science is a natural step for teachers using this approach as you will be used to eliciting information from the children related to your learning objectives. By using this approach to your own understanding of science concepts your own scientific approach will develop more.

> I have a degree in science but I've never been expected to ask questions and answer them. This is the first time I've done this. This is real science!
> (A student teacher talking after a primary science workshop)

## Note – Explanation of the syphon – a useful analogy

Imagine a climber standing at the top of a cliff with a long rope coiled neatly at her feet. What would happen if she gathered up several metres of rope and threw it off the cliff? If she has thrown enough rope, the weight of that rope falling will be sufficient to pull more rope over the edge.

Does this help you with the syphon?

Try to imagine the water in the tube as a 'liquid rope'. Once a given weight of 'liquid rope' (water) is down the pipe and its mass exerting a pulling force (as long as no bubbles of air get into the tube) on the water in the top tank, more water will be pulled into and down the tube. This continues until there is no more water to be pulled or until bubbles of air enter the system.

By now you may have a number of new questions about syphons and objects being dropped off cliffs! Whilst we advocate further investigation we advise caution!

## BIBLIOGRAPHY

Farrow, S. (1996) *The Really Useful Science Book*, London: Falmer Press.

Harlen, W. (1992) *The Teaching of Science*, London: David Fulton.

Nussbaum, J. (1985) The Earth as a cosmic body, in R. Driver, E. Guesne and A. Tiberghien, *Children's Ideas in Science*, Milton Keynes: Open University Press.

Osborne, R. and Freyburg, P. (1985) *Children's Learning in Science*, London: Heinemann.

Smith, R. G. and Peacock, G. (1990) Tackling contradictions in teachers' understanding of gravity and air resistance, in L. Newton, *Primary Science: The Challenge of the 1990s*, Clevedon: Multilingual Matters.

Summers, M. and Kruger, C. (1990) Research into English primary school teachers' understanding of the concept 'energy', in L. Newton, *Primary Science: The Challenge of the 1990s*, Clevedon: Multilingual Matters.

## FURTHER READING

### Science topic

*Electricity*    Shipstone, D. (1985) Electricity in simple circuits, in R. Driver, E. Guesne and A. Tiberghien, *Children's Ideas in Science*, Milton Keynes: Open University Press.

*Light*    Guesne, E. (1985) Light, in R. Driver, E. Guesne and A. Tiberghien, *Children's Ideas in Science*, Milton Keynes: Open University Press.

*Gravity*    Smith and Peacock (see above)

*Earth and space*    Nussbaum (see above)
Bk. 1, Heywood, 3

*Heat and thermal insulation*    Driver, R. (1983) *The Pupil As Scientist*, Milton Keynes: Open University Press.

*Air*    Brook, A. and Driver, R. (1989) *The Development of Pupils' Understanding of Physical Characteristics of Air Across the Age Range 5–16 Years*, Leeds: Children's Learning in Science (CLIS) Project, University of Leeds.

*Others*    Primary SPACE Project: Research Reports: *Growth, Light, Forces, Sound, Electricity, Materials, Energy, Earth and Atmosphere, Earth in Space, Processes of Life, Variety of Life* (various dates) CRIPSAT and King's College, London: Liverpool University Press.

ir definitions through exploring their vocabulary and having their
sting ideas challenged.

Although the process is not an exact one and will vary between
ividuals, some common elements are identifiable within the
mework for language developed in Book 1 (Bk. 1, Heywood, 3).
s includes working from an existing vocabulary acquired from
mon experience (compiling the lists of solids, liquids and gases),
slating the vocabulary into a 'scientific' framework through
erating a definition in more detail as to what the categories mean,
I then finally interpreting those meanings through having ideas
llenged. Such a process which leads to an increasingly sophisticated
rpretation is an integral aspect of learning in science. It is
ortant to provide opportunities beyond simple vocabulary
uisition such that learning words in science progresses beyond a
re labelling process.

### tivity 2 – Messages on paper

me required: 1–2 hours)

s second activity follows on from the previous examination of
ds, liquids and gases. This activity is a piece of classroom action
earch. This simply means that you will give the activity to a group
children, observe and note their responses, and use the data to
strate the implications of language in learning science. This can be
owed later with examples from different age groups in order to
strate issues of progression and development in children's language
I thinking.

'or ease of resources (including teacher time in a crowded
riculum) the example given is focused on work with paper.
member the purpose of the exercise is to raise awareness
I understanding of the use of language in children's learning in
nce.

he activity is based on the work of Parker (1995) and is intended
ocus on the language which children use to describe the properties
paper, a material with which they are familiar. The duration of the
vity can be short but it does require teacher input in terms of
stioning. Using a tape recorder will reduce note-taking but will
uire time to listen to the tape.

rovide the children with a variety of different types of paper
chen roll, tissue, newspaper, brown paper, wrapping paper, etc.),
crumple, stretch, tear and fold. The tactile experience of handling
paper will provide them with an opportunity to describe the
perties through comparing the similarities and differences. Listen

# 3
# Spreading the Message: Exploring Language and Learning in Science

*David Heywood*

## INTRODUCTION

This chapter develops the ideas introduced in the companion book
(Bk. 1, Heywood, 3) addressing the issue of language and learning in
science in a practical way. The practical exploration of the use of
language by teachers and children in developing meaning incorporates
a wide range of activities including reading, writing, discussion,
experimentation and trial and error through active participation. The
purpose of the following interactive examples is to raise awareness of
the key ideas involved and to illustrate the central role of language
in science learning.

The tasks presented are aimed at exploring issues with colleagues
to raise general awareness and ultimately to enhance the quality of
science teaching and learning. Some work is specifically targeted for
children's learning, while many of the practical ideas suggested for
working with colleagues will have direct implications for teaching
tasks. These could, with a little imagination, be adopted for classroom
activities to develop children's ideas in science. It is important to
recognise that the task of interpreting ideas in science is a continuous
one. Some activities can therefore be usefully deployed to develop
meaning at an increasingly sophisticated level.

The first activity is aimed at raising awareness of the process of
interpreting meaning from challenging existing definitions in order to
develop ideas. It is best carried out with a partner or in a small group.

The resource implications for this activity are minimal and useful follow up work for the classroom can be found in Nuffield Primary Science (1995).

## Activity 1 – Change of state! Solid, liquid or gas?

(Time required: 1 hour)

One way of illustrating the importance of how language influences ideas in science is to look more closely at both the definitions and the sorts of ideas associated with a word. The following task is intended to raise awareness of how ideas evolve through challenging existing definitions. The activity can be used as a starting point to illustrate how discussion can provide opportunity for developing our thinking about ideas in science.

Look at these words, think of examples and make lists of:

| Solids | Liquids | Gases |
|--------|---------|-------|

Items listed might include:

| Solids | Liquids | Gases |
|--------|---------|-------|
| wood | water | air |
| metal | petrol | oxygen |
| plastic | paint | carbon dioxide |
| string | bleach | methane |
| wax | oil | hydrogen |

It is worth discussing any of the above which presented difficulty. Which list was the easiest to compile? Gases often present a problem because they are not as perceptible to our senses. Many of them cannot be seen, touched or detected through smell. The list of gases is also different in that it is likely to contain more 'scientific' words outside common everyday language.

Having discussed the lists now consider how you might define each category:

| Solids are: | Liquids are: | Gases are: |
|-------------|--------------|------------|

This activity requires a comparison and contrast between the categories in order to come up with a working definition. The sorts of definitions which are commonly encountered include:

- **Solids**: strong, rigid, hard, stiff, keep their shape, c... light, rough or smooth, opaque or transparent.

- **Liquids**: flow, are weak, heavy, easily change s... difficult to contain.

- **Gases**: very difficult to contain, spread out easily, ... usually can't be seen, light, dangerous, often smel...

It is not important that the definitions contain all of th... but that they clearly distinguish between solids, liquids ... next step in the process is to challenge the definitions ... materials that do not readily fit into the categories ... following list. How do these fit into the categories?

| | |
|----------------|------------------|
| talcum powder | hair gel |
| toothpaste | shaving foam |
| spray paint | spray deodorant |
| Tippex | |

This list is intended to challenge the definitions. For e... powder has some of the characteristics of liquids in tha... up the shape of the container it is in and so on. It is r... does require thinking further about what might cou... Other examples in the list are more difficult. For exan... foam really a combination of liquid and gas? Wou... definition consider that shaving foam is a gas trapped ...

### Recognising the process

The key issue in terms of raising awareness of the role ... learning in science concerns recognising the process ... There are many points which can (and probably will) ... one of which might include the tentative nature of cl... the associated grey areas around the margins of the ... categories are human constructs used to make sense of ... are not definitive; they are open to debate abou... categories can be challenged and reinterpreted throu... and discussion. During such a process the categories ... and gas take on an increasingly sophisticated meani... of the ways in which we develop our understandi... themselves are interpreted in the light of experienc... simply labelling devices. A further extension of thi... encourage colleagues to provide opportunity for pu...

# 3
# Spreading the Message: Exploring Language and Learning in Science

*David Heywood*

## INTRODUCTION

This chapter develops the ideas introduced in the companion book (Bk. 1, Heywood, 3) addressing the issue of language and learning in science in a practical way. The practical exploration of the use of language by teachers and children in developing meaning incorporates a wide range of activities including reading, writing, discussion, experimentation and trial and error through active participation. The purpose of the following interactive examples is to raise awareness of the key ideas involved and to illustrate the central role of language in science learning.

The tasks presented are aimed at exploring issues with colleagues to raise general awareness and ultimately to enhance the quality of science teaching and learning. Some work is specifically targeted for children's learning, while many of the practical ideas suggested for working with colleagues will have direct implications for teaching tasks. These could, with a little imagination, be adopted for classroom activities to develop children's ideas in science. It is important to recognise that the task of interpreting ideas in science is a continuous one. Some activities can therefore be usefully deployed to develop meaning at an increasingly sophisticated level.

The first activity is aimed at raising awareness of the process of interpreting meaning from challenging existing definitions in order to develop ideas. It is best carried out with a partner or in a small group.

The resource implications for this activity are minimal and useful follow up work for the classroom can be found in Nuffield Primary Science (1995).

## Activity 1 – Change of state! Solid, liquid or gas?
(Time required: 1 hour)
One way of illustrating the importance of how language influences ideas in science is to look more closely at both the definitions and the sorts of ideas associated with a word. The following task is intended to raise awareness of how ideas evolve through challenging existing definitions. The activity can be used as a starting point to illustrate how discussion can provide opportunity for developing our thinking about ideas in science.

Look at these words, think of examples and make lists of:

| Solids | Liquids | Gases |
|--------|---------|-------|

Items listed might include:

| Solids | Liquids | Gases |
|--------|---------|-------|
| wood | water | air |
| metal | petrol | oxygen |
| plastic | paint | carbon dioxide |
| string | bleach | methane |
| wax | oil | hydrogen |

It is worth discussing any of the above which presented difficulty. Which list was the easiest to compile? Gases often present a problem because they are not as perceptible to our senses. Many of them cannot be seen, touched or detected through smell. The list of gases is also different in that it is likely to contain more 'scientific' words outside common everyday language.

Having discussed the lists now consider how you might define each category:

| Solids are: | Liquids are: | Gases are: |
|-------------|--------------|------------|

This activity requires a comparison and contrast between the categories in order to come up with a working definition. The sorts of definitions which are commonly encountered include:

24

- **Solids**: strong, rigid, hard, stiff, keep their shape, can be heavy or light, rough or smooth, opaque or transparent.

- **Liquids**: flow, are weak, heavy, easily change shape, smooth, difficult to contain.

- **Gases**: very difficult to contain, spread out easily, move rapidly, usually can't be seen, light, dangerous, often smell.

It is not important that the definitions contain all of the above words but that they clearly distinguish between solids, liquids and gases. The next step in the process is to challenge the definitions by introducing materials that do not readily fit into the categories. Consider the following list. How do these fit into the categories?

| | |
|---|---|
| talcum powder | hair gel |
| toothpaste | shaving foam |
| spray paint | spray deodorant |
| Tippex | |

This list is intended to challenge the definitions. For example, talcum powder has some of the characteristics of liquids in that it flows, takes up the shape of the container it is in and so on. It is not a liquid but does require thinking further about what might count for a liquid. Other examples in the list are more difficult. For example, is shaving foam really a combination of liquid and gas? Would a workable definition consider that shaving foam is a gas trapped in a liquid?

## Recognising the process

The key issue in terms of raising awareness of the role of language in learning in science concerns recognising the process within the task. There are many points which can (and probably will) be raised here, one of which might include the tentative nature of classification and the associated grey areas around the margins of the categories. The categories are human constructs used to make sense of materials. They are not definitive; they are open to debate about whether the categories can be challenged and reinterpreted through questioning and discussion. During such a process the categories of solid, liquid and gas take on an increasingly sophisticated meaning. This is one of the ways in which we develop our understanding. The words themselves are interpreted in the light of experience; they are not simply labelling devices. A further extension of this process is to encourage colleagues to provide opportunity for pupils to develop their definitions through exploring their vocabulary and having their existing ideas challenged.

Although the process is not an exact one and will vary between individuals, some common elements are identifiable within the framework for language developed in Book 1 (Bk. 1, Heywood, 3). This includes working from an existing vocabulary acquired from common experience (compiling the lists of solids, liquids and gases), translating the vocabulary into a 'scientific' framework through generating a definition in more detail as to what the categories mean, and then finally interpreting those meanings through having ideas challenged. Such a process which leads to an increasingly sophisticated interpretation is an integral aspect of learning in science. It is important to provide opportunities beyond simple vocabulary acquisition such that learning words in science progresses beyond a mere labelling process.

### Activity 2 – Messages on paper

(Time required: 1–2 hours)
This second activity follows on from the previous examination of solids, liquids and gases. This activity is a piece of classroom action research. This simply means that you will give the activity to a group of children, observe and note their responses, and use the data to illustrate the implications of language in learning science. This can be followed later with examples from different age groups in order to illustrate issues of progression and development in children's language and thinking.

For ease of resources (including teacher time in a crowded curriculum) the example given is focused on work with paper. Remember the purpose of the exercise is to raise awareness and understanding of the use of language in children's learning in science.

The activity is based on the work of Parker (1995) and is intended to focus on the language which children use to describe the properties of paper, a material with which they are familiar. The duration of the activity can be short but it does require teacher input in terms of questioning. Using a tape recorder will reduce note-taking but will require time to listen to the tape.

Provide the children with a variety of different types of paper (kitchen roll, tissue, newspaper, brown paper, wrapping paper, etc.), to crumple, stretch, tear and fold. The tactile experience of handling the paper will provide them with an opportunity to describe the properties through comparing the similarities and differences. Listen

26

carefully to the words they use to describe the papers and use the matrix below to record the most common adjectives:

---

**Words most frequently used:** (likely to include rough, smooth, soft, weak, strong)

**Words often used**: (could include stretchy, bendy, stiff, absorbent)

**Words seldom used**: (might include delicate, flexible, springy, slippery)

---

To develop the list, encourage the children to think about how paper behaves when handled in particular ways. This might include setting challenges such as:

- Will the paper fold without tearing?

- Is the paper easily squashed?

- Does the paper soak up water?

- Will the paper stretch?

- What happens when you tear the paper?

In discussion with the children try to establish how the children relate the tactile experience to the words they use to describe the paper. For example, do they associate the word 'strong' with paper that is difficult to tear? Or is the word 'weak' used to describe paper which is thin? It is possible that the descriptive words refer to the known intended function of the paper so that the word 'absorbent' is used for kitchen towels because they are used to wipe up spillages or brown paper is 'strong' because it is used for parcelling. It is likely that such discussion with the children will reveal a wide variety of reasons for describing paper in a particular way, not all of which will be easily categorised.

### Challenging our assumptions
There are two important questions to consider:

- Do children sometimes use the same word to describe different things?

- Do children sometimes use different words to describe the same thing?

This is an important aspect of both teaching and learning in science. How often do we assume that we are using words in the same way without challenging that assumption? Parker (1995) revealed some interesting findings when working with children in this area with respect to the use of the word 'strong'. Other research (Russell and Watt, 1991) has revealed the importance of providing children with the opportunity to explore the meanings of the words they use. Children often derive the meaning of a word from experiences in particular contexts. In the above example they might well consider that 'strong' and 'weak' are not words they would apply to paper because they think of paper as a material used for wrapping parcels or for drawing on. The implications for this in a practical investigation on the strength of paper would be highly significant if the children are not afforded the opportunity to explore the use of the word in such a context. Clearly there is a need for the teacher to seek clarification as to a common agreement in the use of the words in order to secure a reasonable consensus as to their interpretation.

The question then arises as to how best to use the data collected from this particular piece of classroom research. There are several possible ways in which this can be used effectively to raise staff awareness of the language issues involved. It is important to be selective but some of the following are ways in which you might consider using the data.

### Activity 3 – Using the classroom data
(Time required: 1 hour)
Explore the range of vocabulary used. Were you surprised by:

- the number of words the children used?

- the limited range of words used by the children?

- the words themselves?

- any omissions?

Focus on the way children interpreted the words to illustrate the significance of:

● providing children with the opportunity to discuss their ideas;

● clarifying with children their interpretation of the words they are using;

● the role of practical investigation which provides children with an opportunity to relate the descriptions they use to tactile experience.

## Extending the work

In raising these issues from the work with your children you have created a useful platform to extend the work towards incorporating a wider range of examples. These might include pupils of different age ranges, which would mean more opportunity to involve colleagues in this investigation with their own pupils. Teachers all need support in planning effectively and you can use the framework from your own classroom practice to illustrate the importance of focusing on the language in such an activity. A very important element of this concerns the role of the teacher as questioner and listener.

There are likely to be a number of concerns raised with regard to this, particularly the time required in order to carry out small group and individual activities. Such approaches impact upon classroom organisation and resources. If you involve colleagues you should be prepared for questions which may arise about the nature of learning in science or the way the National Curriculum is planned and delivered. This can lead to insecurity if not handled sensitively in a professional manner. It is all the more important to stress the purpose of the exercise, that it is intended to start off a debate to raise awareness as to the impact of language in learning science which is often in conflict with our everyday use of vocabulary.

One way of extending this is by collecting a portfolio of work completed by pupils in specific areas of science. The exercise should not take up too much time and the data collected will provide a wealth of material which can be used for future planning, INSET and assessment activities. Over the course of a year a small number of conceptual areas could be looked at. It might also contribute insight into the range of approaches to 'Experimental and Investigative Science'. The role of language is as important in 'Experimental and Investigative Science' as it is in all aspects of science understanding. Investigations provide a means to develop vocabulary and to enable more sophisticated ideas to evolve.

## Activity 4 – Towards shared meaning

(Time required: 1 hour)

This activity is designed to illustrate the significance of using the same vocabulary to describe the same things. If we are talking the 'same language' then we have a greater chance of developing our thinking and ideas about certain concepts. The activity is intended for colleagues but can be easily adapted for work in the classroom.

Examine some common objects or structural materials as follows:

| Object | Material |
|--------|----------|
| glove | woven wool |
| table | wood |
| elastic band | rubber |
| paper clip | steel |
| coffee mug | ceramic |
| blown egg | eggshell |
| a mock parcel | string and paper |
| old tap | copper and chrome |
| washing up bottle | polythene |
| pan scourer | wire wool or nylon |

Pose the questions:

● What is the object used for?

● What material is it made from?

● What is it about the material that makes it particularly suitable for the job?

Listen carefully to the discussions as the lists are made. Compile a common list from feedback from the activity. This is likely to result in numerous adjectives; for example, strong, weak, absorbent, coloured, cheap, synthetic, strong, large, tough, curved, fibrous, stretchy, bendy, stiff, rough, smooth, etc. Some of the words refer to the structure and shape of the object, and others refer to the material from which the object is made.

### Comparisons, measurements and definitions

The question arises as to how a material is judged to be strong or tough. This is presumably derived from a comparison to other materials which are not strong or tough. Comparisons in this instance are subjectively made, based on our personal experiences. What I consider to be tough could be interpreted entirely differently by a colleague. More importantly, when you refer to toughness, you could be considering a property of the material that another might interpret as strength. For the purposes of clarifying what we mean by strong we need a measurement to compare a strong material with a weak one. In order to do this we must be clear about an agreed definition of the property of strength. Materials scientists have worked on this and a definition adapted from Gordon (1991) defines the **strength** of a material as the amount of force needed to break the material in two. **Tensile strength** is the amount of force needed to pull the material apart. Because a thicker sample is going to be stronger than a thinner one of the same material, we need to have a standard size for the purpose of comparison. So that we have a fair test, the tensile strength is defined as the force needed to break a bar of 1 $cm^2$ cross-section. The definitions in Table 3.1 are in themselves only meaningful if we can relate them to our personal experiences.

**Table 3.1. Definitions of properties of materials**

| Property of material | Definition |
| --- | --- |
| *Strength* | The amount of force needed to break a material in two. Tensile strength is the amount of force needed to pull the material apart. Because a thicker sample will be stronger than a thinner one made of the same material the tensile strength of a material is defined as the force needed to break a bar of 1 $cm^2$ cross-section. |
| *Elasticity* | The extent to which something goes back to its original shape and size when a force exerted upon it is released. |
| *Plasticity* | The extent to which an object stays in the shape that you put it in. |
| *Stiffness* | The resistance a material has to having its shape changed. |
| *Hardness* | The difficulty of scratching, wearing away or denting a material. |

| | |
|---|---|
| *Brittleness* | Refers to the way a material breaks. Both strong and weak materials can be brittle if they break shattering into pieces, rather than by pulling apart gradually. |
| *Toughness* | The opposite of brittleness. It is the property of toffee that means you can bend it backwards and forwards almost forever and it still won't break. |
| *Absorbency* | The amount of liquid soaked up by a certain area or volume of the material. |

We can have tactile experience of many of the properties of a material as defined in this way. For example, there are some materials that are easily stretched and revert back to their original shape while others do not. We could refer to this property as 'stetchability' or 'pliability' since these are reasonable descriptions of materials such as rubber bands. However, materials which are less evidently stretchy or pliable do have this property which can be measured in certain conditions. For the purposes of comparison, a single word is required which describes this singular property. That word is 'elasticity'.

Some materials have a combination of properties which enable us to distinguish between them. 'Stiffness' might be referred to in describing steel since it is resistant to having its shape changed, but so is a biscuit! The two materials are clearly not the same. Steel is stiff and strong, a biscuit is stiff but weak. The difference in strength provides us with a means of comparison. Similarly, a nylon thread could be described as being flexible and strong whereas a strip of BluTack would be flexible but weak.

The descriptors help us make sense of the properties of a material and to determine their most appropriate uses. It is through exploring the interpretation of the words used to describe the properties that we begin to make sense of the materials themselves. In this process we are then more able to understand the suitability of materials for particular purposes. This helps us make the conceptual link between the properties of materials and their uses. The interpretations evolve through experience rather than as a static outcome of the process. What is needed is an open and honest discourse which enables children to derive meaning from the words.

## CONCLUSIONS

The activities described above are all intended to raise our professional awareness of how language is integral to learning in science. It is not simply a case of acquiring new vocabulary at appropriate points in our learning. Neither is it a question of absolute specific definitions of particular words in particular contexts. Rote learning of specific definitions is unlikely to enable understanding of the ideas encountered. There is the issue of the way certain words are used in science compared to their everyday common use. For example, children use the word 'energy' in a quite different way from how scientists use the word. Working towards a shared, 'scientific' meaning through discussion, reading and practical activity is more meaningful than memorising the definition of the word. Thus we require that everyday experience be used to articulate scientific definition so that learners can make links between new and existing ideas.

We need to recognise as teachers of science in the primary years that the key issue is one of interpretation rather than acquisition and that interpretation is constantly evolving. This evolution takes time, perhaps the most scarce commodity in a crowded curriculum! Teachers need to appreciate the value of developing children's thinking through exploring their own definitions and interpretations in science.

### Acknowledgment

The author would like to express his thanks to colleagues Joan Parker and Frank Gibson for their assistance in checking the accuracy of terminology used in the text.

### BIBLIOGRAPHY

Gordon, J. E. (1991) *Structures Or Why Things Don't Fall Down*, London: Penguin.

Nuffield Primary Science (1995) *Materials – Teachers Guide KS2* (and other titles), London: Collins.

Parker, J. (1995) Words on paper, *Primary Science Review*, no. 36, February.

Russell, T. and Watt, D. (1991) *Evaporation and Condensation – Primary SPACE Research Project Report*, Liverpool University Press.

Sutton, C. (1992) *Words Science and Learning*, Buckinghamshire: Open University Press.

# 4
# Progression and Differentiation in Science: Some General Strategies

*Stuart Naylor and Brenda Keogh*

## WHY ARE GENERAL STRATEGIES RELEVANT?

In this chapter some general strategies for promoting progression and differentiation are suggested; in the following chapter progression and differentiation are considered separately.

One reason for this is that many teachers and researchers believe that difficult issues such as progression and differentiation are more effectively handled as whole-school issues. This is preferable to such strategies being utilised by individual teachers alone with individual children (Stradling, Saunders and Weston, 1991). Progression and differentiation are so important to education that they must be considered alongside other factors which affect learning. There seems little point devoting your energies to the mechanics and detail of progression and differentiation in a subject like science without first looking at more general questions of the extent to which the curriculum and learning situation are suited to the children.

A second reason is that progression and differentiation are intimately connected. The purpose of providing differentiated learning experiences for children is to promote more effective progression in their learning. The kinds of strategies that make differentiation more effective will, therefore, lead to better progression in learning.

34

# CHILDREN'S INDEPENDENCE AS LEARNERS

Children's independence as learners is particularly important for promoting differentiation and progression in learning. When children are working as independent learners, this creates circumstances in which teachers can interact more effectively with the children. It also helps the children to take a greater share of the responsibility for their learning.

## Indicators of independence

Independence in learning must permeate the whole curriculum. It should not be restricted to science but rather be promoted by science teaching. It will be possible to identify indicators of independence generally. Others are more likely to occur when the children are working on science-based activities.

General indicators of independence in learning include:

- children making decisions about the nature and content of their learning;

- children making decisions about the organisation of their learning;

- children making decisions about resources to support their learning and having access to these resources;

- children being expected to make their own judgments about the quality of their learning;

- children being self-motivated and self-directed in learning activities.

In addition to these general opportunities to display independence in their learning, science presents children with some specific opportunities. More science-specific indicators of independence in learning might include the ability to:

- understand the problem and define the task;

- create effective plans to solve the problem;

- make use of information and ideas in planning;

- change the procedure to make it more effective;

- choose sensible methods for recording information.

35

## Making judgments about independence in learning

In order to make progress with independence in learning the school needs to make a judgment about current practice. The indicators listed can help in this review process. Individual teachers could reflect on which of these indicators are observed in their classrooms; the staff as a whole could reflect on their overall impression of the children, including how they behave outside formal lesson times; one teacher (including the headteacher) could act as an internal consultant and provide feedback on independence in learning to the rest of the staff.

Reflecting on these indicators will allow the school to make a judgment about how independent the children are as learners. Making a judgment can then lead to a decision about the need for further development in this area.

## Making independence in learning more likely

If a school identifies concerns about the extent of the children's independent behaviour, what can be done to improve the situation? If independence in learning is a whole-school, whole-curriculum issue, desired change is unlikely to come from single actions or strategies. Instead, the desired change is more likely to be effected by a combination of actions or strategies.

Some suggestions for making independence in learning more likely are:

- use the children's ideas as the starting point for learning;

- value the children's ideas;

- establish classroom routines that provide support for the children to operate independently, e.g. using charts or work diaries to make the sequence of activities visible to the children;

- provide ready access to well-organised resources;

- have other tasks available that the children can turn to when they have finished one activity;

- make sure that the children know what the point of the activity is;

- negotiate activities with the children;

- give the children real responsibilities in the classroom;

- allow the children to make mistakes and ensure that they learn from them;

- teach the children the skills that they need to be ab effectively without input from the teacher;

- introduce greater independence gradually.

Independence in learning is itself an important objective. In this chapter, however, we are considering it as a means to an end. Greater independence will normally lead to better differentiation and progression in learning. The priorities for independence are therefore concerned with children's overall role in the classroom and shared responsibility for their learning rather than with the specific details of classroom organisation.

## LEARNING STYLE

Teachers will be familiar with the idea that different children learn best in different ways. While some prefer to talk about the subject of their learning, others find that text is more useful to them. Some prefer to work individually while others are happier in a group. Some children are most confident when they have detailed instructions to follow while others prefer the challenge of an open-ended problem. Some appear to learn very little without first-hand experience while others can manipulate abstract ideas more successfully.

These differences in the children's learning styles are part of everyday life for teachers. One implication of these differences is that where a narrow range of teaching styles is employed some children are likely to be taught ineffectively. This would lead to a risk that some children will be seriously disadvantaged in their learning. The wider the range of styles a teacher has experienced and can select and use effectively, the more likely it is that all the children will be adequately catered for.

### Reviewing the range of teaching/learning strategies used

Individual teachers can reflect on the range of strategies that they use in their teaching. Which strategies are used frequently? Which are used occasionally? Which are not used at all? A list of possible strategies can serve as a useful checklist to support this review process. One such list is shown below. Teachers may well wish to add other strategies to the list.

- solving a problem;

- planning and carrying out an investigation;

- making observations and deciding what they mean;
- following an individual workcard;
- practising a technique or skill;
- researching using text or CD ROM;
- discussing in small groups;
- whole-class discussion;
- long-term individual project;
- making a model;
- producing a model;
- producing a display;
- watching a video;
- going on a trip or visit;
- teacher talking or reading to the children;
- writing down ideas.

After reviewing the teaching/learning strategies that they use some teachers may decide that it is necessary to adjust the approaches used in their teaching. The decision will be based on whether all of the children are being catered for adequately with the range of approaches used at present.

One possibility might be to use a broader range of teaching/learning strategies. Another might be to use certain approaches more frequently, possibly for particular types of subject content or for particular children.

## Making decisions about which teaching/learning strategies to use

Using a broad range of teaching/learning strategies is more likely to create the circumstances in which progression and differentiation are achieved. How could teachers go further and make decisions about when to use a particular approach?

The circumstances at the time will be an important factor in this decision. How independent, well-motivated or well-behaved the children are will allow certain possibilities and exclude others. Similarly the resources available will be important, including the space, the amount of time and whether there is any support from other adults. The nature of the subject matter that the children are learning will also make a difference to the choice of teaching/learning approaches. Decisions will have to be made about whether the teaching should be individual or group-based; teacher-led or pupil-led; hands-on; talk- or text-based, and so on.

Where a teacher knows a group of children particularly well it may be possible to take the learning styles of individual children into account in planning activities. It may therefore be that while the learning objectives may be similar the approach to a topic may be different for different children. This may only be possible where a teacher has worked with a class for a considerable period and where the class size is not unreasonably large. Such approaches are most often possible where a teacher has adult assistance. This ought to increase the opportunity for the teacher to interact with individual children. Records that give some indication of the children's individual learning styles will be helpful for the next teacher. However, while taking children's individual learning styles into account is a reasonbale aim, it is unreasonable to expect teachers to do so 100 per cent of the time.

Another possibility is to find out the children's preferred learning styles and to take these into account in planning activities. This could involve providing children with a simple list of possible teaching/learning approaches and getting them to review how they feel they learn best, possibly by scoring each one or placing them in rank order. Using this approach would require the teacher to acknowledge the children's preferences. Teachers might then consider a degree of negotiation with the children in some activities about how children could choose to tackle them.

## SCIENTIFIC PROCEDURAL SKILLS

The way that children use the skills of scientific investigation is also relevant to progression and to differentiation. This can be an important aspect of differentiation in science, since the level of demand of an activity can be adjusted through the scientific procedure to be used as well as through the science concepts involved. It is an important aspect of progression in learning science, since developing understanding in science depends on the ability to test ideas in a scientific manner (Harlen, 1993).

Details of the various skills involved in working scientifically and how progression in each of these might be recognised are given in

Goldsworthy and Feasey (1994). However, planning for progression in the use of specific skills with each child is unrealistic in most situations. A more realistic approach is to attempt to raise the children's awareness of what it means to work scientifically. In this way the children will be most likely to be using their procedural capabilities to the full and will increasingly take the initiative in determining the scientific procedure to be used.

Details of the teacher's role in raising awareness of how to use a scientific approach are given in Jarman, Keogh and Naylor (1994). The teacher's role can include:

● providing opportunities for children to explore and investigate;

● helping children to see the purpose of their explorations and investigations;

● encouraging children to plan before doing;

● encouraging children to explain what they are doing and why;

● keeping the purpose of the investigation in mind at all stages;

● emphasising all aspects of the procedure, not just fair testing;

● teaching the children specific skills and techniques;

● providing examples of other children's work to illustrate suitable approaches;

● reflecting on the process and the content of the investigation;

● valuing the children's efforts to work scientifically.

Using lists such as these it is possible for individuals or groups of teachers to reflect on their own practice and to make judgments about which of these aspects of the teacher's role are presently employed. This can lead on to decisions about how practice may need to be modified. In this way the children's awareness of how to work scientifically may be enhanced.

## DEVELOPING A WHOLE-SCHOOL APPROACH TO TEACHING AND LEARNING

A whole-school approach to teaching and learning will ensure that the children get a reasonably consistent experience from any of the teachers in the school. It will promote continuity in the teaching and learning approaches used from class to class.

Clearly it is not possible to specify every aspect of teaching and learning that might be used in a whole-school approach. Even if it were, teachers would find that their freedom to develop their own individual style would be too restricted. Instead, schools ought to aim to identify the aspects of teaching and learning which they feel are most important. They should then work towards developing a whole-school approach to these priority aspects.

**Reflecting on practice**
This is best achieved through discussion, either with the whole staff or in smaller groups. The aim of the discussion should be to attempt to describe the approaches to teaching and learning which are normally used throughout the school. Although it is possible for individual teachers to reflect on their own practice, lack of opportunity for discussion can seriously restrict people's thinking.

A whole-school approach to teaching and learning is likely to involve specifying some aspects of the nature of learning activities, the pupils' role, the teacher's role and the learning environment. Each of these will have a bearing on progression and differentiation. Some questions to guide discussion are provided, though schools may have different priorities from those listed.

*Active learning*
- Do all teachers use a wide range of approaches to learning?

- Is the purpose for activities always clear to the children?

- Is there an emphasis on thinking as well as an emphasis on doing?

- Are the children encouraged to suggest how they might go about an activity?

*Children as independent learners (described in more detail above)*
- What choices do children make about their learning?

- Do they have independent access to resources?

- Are children encouraged to be responsible for their own learning?

- Are children taught the necessary skills to enable them to operate as independent learners?

● Are children encouraged to evaluate their own work?

*Questioning style*
● Do all teachers use a range of questioning styles?

● Are questions mostly about organisation and procedures, or are they designed to challenge the children's thinking?

● What proportion of questions are productive questions (see Harlen, 1985) which lead on to investigations or further work by the children?

● Is there positive reinforcement for children's answers?

● Are the children's questions encouraged and valued?

*Learning environment*
● Are children always in the same group, or is grouping more flexible?

● Are other children seen as useful resources for learning?

● Do children sit together and work independently, or are they required to work together on collaborative tasks?

● To what extent is talk seen as an important part of learning?

**Deciding what kind of development may be needed**
Through reflection on present teaching and learning approaches, using the questions above or some other systematic aid to reflection, it becomes possible to see what kinds of development might need to go on. To what extent does current practice help to achieve the school's overall goals for learning? To what extent do staff use similar approaches to teaching and learning? The discussion should allow staff to identify any concerns about the children's learning. These concerns can then be analysed to try to identify why they arise and how they might be avoided.

An alternative, more positive approach could be to identify what is working well and to build on this good practice. This would involve teachers in:

● identifying some learning activities which they feel have been successful;

● reflecting on what seemed significant about the teaching and learning approach in making the activity successful;

● sharing their ideas about successful approaches;

● agreeing which aspects of teaching and learning frequently seem to be involved in successful activities;

● considering how these aspects can be incorporated into day-to-day practice by all staff.

## Working towards a whole-school approach

Developing a common approach to teaching and learning is likely to require some or all of the teaching staff to modify their practice. This may not be easy. It will be necessary for all the staff to have a clear idea of what developments they are working towards and how this will help the school's overall goals for learning to be achieved. It is important not to be overambitious. Taking one or two aspects of teaching and learning, considering these in some detail and working towards a more consistent approach in those areas is a realistic strategy. When these have been addressed to people's satisfaction then the list can be extended.

At some point it will be useful to produce a whole-school teaching and learning policy. The purpose of having a policy is to identify clearly the common values, intentions and commitments of the staff for teaching and learning throughout the school. A policy can also help to document the progress that the school has made. The process of producing the policy can in itself be a useful stimulus to staff development and curriculum development. Ultimately a policy should represent a whole-school commitment to adopting a particular approach to teaching and learning.

## BIBLIOGRAPHY

Goldsworthy, A. and Feasey, R. (1994) *Making Sense of Primary Science Investigations*, Hatfield: Association for Science Education.
Harlen, W. (ed) (1985) *Primary Science: Taking the Plunge*, London: Heinemann.
Harlen, W. (1993) Children's learning in science, in R. Sherrington (ed) *ASE Primary Science Teachers' Handbook*, Hemel Hempstead: Simon and Schuster.
Jarman, R., Keogh, B. and Naylor, S. (1994) *I've Done This Before: Continuity and Progression in School Science*, Hatfield: Association for Science Education.
Stradling, R., Saunders, L. with Weston, P. (1991) *Differentiation in Action: a Whole-School Approach to Raising Attainment*, London: HMSO.

# 5
# Progression and Differentiation in Science: Some Specific Strategies

*Stuart Naylor and Brenda Keogh*

## INTRODUCTION

In this chapter some specific strategies for promoting progression and differentiation in science are suggested. This chapter has been written to follow on from the previous one and our chapters in the companion book (Bk. 1, Naylor and Keogh, 4 and 5). The strategies suggested will be of little value if they are used in isolation. It is important to make their use part of a whole-school approach.

## PROGRESSION

### A framework for sequencing scientific ideas, skills and activities

As discussed in Book 1 (Bk. 1, Naylor and Keogh, 4 and 5), we recognise that it is very difficult for teachers to identify detailed sequences of ideas which map progression in particular concepts. It is generally accepted that learning in science is not linear, which adds complication to planning for progression in conceptual understanding in science. Figure 5.1 shows a framework for sequencing scientific ideas, skills and activities. This framework is intended to provide an overview of how scientific ideas might develop. This can help in planning for progression by giving some indication of the types of experiences which might be suitable for particular learners.

Using the example of ice, which is shown in the final column of Figure 5.1, for very young children much of the work in developing understanding of the factors affecting the change of state of ice is likely to be within the first three stages of the framework which focus on exploration. However, through these early explorations it is possible that some children will reveal that they have a good awareness of these factors and are therefore ready to progress to the next stage of looking at them in a more systematic way.

If you work with older primary children, exploration will remain an important aspect of developing understanding of the concept. However, for children to progress in their understanding most of them will need to be encouraged to engage in systematic investigations. They will need to consider factors more carefully, including quantification where appropriate. In order to progress, some children may also be ready for more abstract ideas which cannot be learnt through their own investigations.

Through your knowledge of the children in your class you may be aware that children might be ready for the next stage and use the framework to plan for this in advance of the lesson. Alternatively, you might adjust the activity as you observe how the children respond in their initial explorations. Being aware of the basic elements of the general framework could help you to make decisions about how to build progressive sequences of work.

You may often find that the same starting activity will be appropriate for all of the children and that it is the nature of their investigations which leads to progression.

An example of questions based on the framework, which could help in planning for progression in understanding of concepts, is given in Figure 5.2.

**Activity 1 – reviewing practice using this framework**
(a) Consider an area of science which you are about to teach. How could this area be developed in relation to the different stages of the framework? (Try to work through the framework to a stage beyond that which you think is relevant for your children.) Will one starter activity be appropriate for all the children? Do you think that any of your children will need to start at a different stage? Do you have resources available to enable some of your children to progress to the next stage if you feel this is necessary as you observe them responding to the activity? Are any of your

| GENERAL FRAMEWORK | THE TEACHER'S ROLE | THE PUPIL'S ROLE | AN ILLUSTRATION |
|---|---|---|---|
| Ideas emerge as generalisations from experience. | Provide opportunities to experience phenomena and talk about them. | Something happens – I see what happens or someone helps me to see. I look more closely – Have I seen what is really happening? | Ice melts. It feels cold, it feels wet . . . the outside melts first. |
| Exploring further. Thinking and talking, beginning to search for patterns. | Provide opportunities to explore ideas further . . . encourage closer observation, thinking and talking, and the beginnings of searching for patterns. | Does it always happen the same? Can I change what happens or can I see something making it change? | Sometimes it melts faster. I can warm it up. I can wrap it up. |
| Asking why – attempting to explain. | Helping the pupils to raise questions and search for possible explanations. | Why does it happen? Can I explain what I think? | When it was near the radiator it melted faster. When I wrapped it in newspaper it did not melt as fast. |
| Using ideas to guide more systematic investigation. | Help pupils to use a more scientific approach to enable them to develop their ideas. | What do I think makes a difference? Can I change what happens in a systematic way so that I really find out what matters? | It seems to be something to do with being warmer or stopping it getting warm. I can measure the temperature, the time, etc. I can try to identify variables. |
| Further investigation<br>– predicting<br>– testing<br>– applying | Help pupils to confirm or challenge their ideas through hypothesising, predicting, testing and applying, quantifying where necessary. | Can I try it in other ways and get the same pattern of results? | I will use bigger blocks of ice/higher temperature/lower temperature/different insulation, etc. |

| Scientific ideas and skills | Activities | Can I...? | Pupil statements |
|---|---|---|---|
| Asking questions identifies the need for further information and more abstract ideas:<br>– from the learner<br>– from some other source (e.g. the teacher) | Provide challenges which help the pupils to see that explanations in observable terms may not be enough.<br><br>encourage the search for abstract ideas, provide access to sources of information | Can I explain what is happening in observable terms?<br><br>Is there more I can find out or you can tell me to help me to understand more about why it happens? | The higher the temperature – the faster it takes to melt. More insulation – slower melting.<br><br>You tell me about particles. I read a book with more information about solids, liquids and gases (I am unlikely to discover atoms on my own). |
| Acquiring and using more abstract concepts. | Provide illustrations and opportunities to apply new abstract ideas. | Can I use what I know to explain what is happening in non-observable terms? | I can now explain melting, using what I know about particles, and explain why the temperature makes a difference. |
| Systematic inquiry involving hypothesising and testing: describing and testing possible applications. | Provide opportunities for more systematic inquiry involving these abstract ideas, including possible applications. | Can I use the idea to explain other changes? | I realise that condensation, freezing and evaporation all use the same theory. |
| Building up relationships between abstract concepts. | Provide illustration and opportunities to relate their learning to other abstract concepts | Can I use the idea to explain a greater range of events? | I can explain ice floating (volume and density) and think about the possible arrangement of particles. |

Fig. 5.1. A framework for sequencing scientific ideas, skills and activities (from Jarman, Keogh and Naylor, 1994).

| QUESTIONS TO GUIDE PLANNING (BASED ON THE FRAMEWORK) | PLANNING FOR KEY STAGE 1 PUPILS USING FLOATING AND SINKING AS AN EXAMPLE |
|---|---|
| • Do the pupils need the opportunity to experience a broad range of phenomena? | Provide a range of objects and materials to observe and explore when placed in water. |
| • Do the pupils need the opportunity to explore their ideas and look for patterns? | Encourage pupils to explore their ideas, e.g. through sorting activities, making predictions about new objects, by trying to alter the way that things float or sink. |
| • Do the pupils need the opportunity to turn their explorations into more focused investigations? | Encourage pupils to ask questions which extend their explorations into investigations, e.g. do all the large things sink? |
| • Do the pupils need the opportunity to investigate a range of ideas in a systematic way, e.g. by quantifying, by using previous knowledge and understanding, by predicting? | Encourage more systematic investigations, eg comparing a range of objects of the same size, same shape, same type of material, etc to compare how well they float or sink. |
| • Do the pupils need access to abstract ideas to take their thinking further? How will they get access to these ideas? | e.g. the relationship between volume and weight: the distinction between the object and what it is made from; the idea of 'heavy for its size' – it is likely that these ideas will only be suitable for very able KS1 pupils. |
| • Are they ready for systematic investigation using abstract ideas and for relating these ideas to other concepts? | Not normally appropriate for these pupils. |

Fig. 5.2. An example of questions to guide planning
(from Jarman, Keogh & Naylor 1994)

children to progress to the next stage if you feel this is necessary as you observe them responding to the activity? Are any of your children likely to need access to abstract ideas? How will you make these available to the children (e.g. books, CD ROM, tell them, etc.)?

(b) Think of examples of children in your class who have been struggling to understand an idea or who have been insufficiently challenged. How can the framework help you to modify activities for these children?

For example, a class of early years children might be learning about sound by playing with, and talking about, musical instruments. Children who show perceptive observations of what is happening when instruments are played might be challenged to look for patterns in their observations and be encouraged to work more independently to begin to predict and explore what makes a difference to the sound an instrument makes.

(c) The framework could be used by a group of staff to consider progression of ideas throughout a school by identifying questions, challenges, activities and resources which might relate to the different stages of the framework for particular concepts. This could help to avoid repetition of experiences, provide support for teachers in their planning and help with recording. As the framework relates development in scientific concepts to development of scientific skills, these discussions should also help to support progression in scientific skills.

## Eliciting and developing children's ideas

It is widely accepted that the ideas which learners currently hold play an important part in their future learning. In order to enable progression to occur it is important that these ideas are taken into account. This issue is discussed in more detail in the companion book (Bk. 1, Naylor and Keogh, 4).

In a typical classroom situation it is not realistic to identify all the ideas which your children hold prior to planning follow-up activities. A more realistic approach is to look for ways of enabling children to make their ideas explicit by using activities which also provide opportunities for them to develop their ideas.

You may be concerned that you are not aware of all the ideas being expressed by your children. Although this would be ideal, it is not essential. Part of the value of eliciting the children's ideas is that they are encouraged to become aware of their own ideas and those of other children in the group. The challenge to their thinking therefore comes from a range of sources. Your role is to provide challenges, to introduce new ideas and more scientifically acceptable ideas when these are appropriate, and to help to summarise ideas at the end of sessions. This final aspect is an important part of planning for progression in conceptual understanding.

In our experience many teachers pay less attention to planning for the final reviewing of ideas and as a consequence do not leave sufficient time for this at the end of lessons. This can often lead to teachers concluding lessons by simply giving children the 'right' answer without making any connection with the ideas currently held by the children and failing to recognise that many of the children might not be ready for the particular idea being presented. The opportunity for further challenge or confirmation of ideas may be lost, and children can leave the lesson with two sets of ideas, those of the teacher and those which they really believe.

In this section some teaching strategies will be discussed in detail. Each one can motivate learners to discuss their ideas, providing opportunities for challenging and developing as well as eliciting their ideas.

## Activity 2 – true/false statements

These can be used at the start of an area of study to promote discussion of ideas and to generate follow-up investigations. The children are given a list of statements about a particular area and they are asked to say whether the statements are true/false/dependent on something else/unsure. The children are given the opportunity to discuss the statements with each other and to carry out investigations where appropriate. It is important to choose the statements bearing in mind the abilities of the group and the specific aspects of the concept which are to be explored.

Examples of true/false statements based on the area of electricity are given below. These examples were produced for 8- and 9-year-old children who have already had some experience of electricity. They are aimed at developing understanding the Programme of Study for SC4 1 a, b, c (DfE, 1995).

● All circuits need a switch.

● All circuits need two wires, a bulb and a battery.

● Switches can be made out of plastic.

- You can put a knot in the wire instead of a switch as it will stop the electricity.

- You can make a circuit with two bulbs where one bulb will stay lit when you take the other one out.

- It does not matter how many bulbs you put in a circuit, they will still shine just as brightly.

- To make a bulb shine more brightly you need to use thicker wire.

- To make a bulb shine more brightly you can turn the battery round the other way.

## Activity 3 – Sorting and Classifying

In order to sort or classify any group of objects it is necessary for the children to make use of their understanding of the particular criteria being used. Where children are asked to identify their own ways of grouping, the sophistication of the selection of their categories for classification will also reveal something of their understanding of the concept being explored. During the processes of sorting and classifying, children may find that they need to modify their ideas to take into account new bits of information or ideas from other learners or their teacher. In this way there is the potential for the children's ideas to be made explicit and to be challenged within the same experience.

Examples of sorting and classifying activities could include pictures of animals and plants: animals including fish, birds, reptiles, etc. as well as mammals; examples of solids, liquids and gases; or different types of soil. Can you see opportunities for this approach in your present or planned science?

## Activity 4 – Predict, observe, explain (POE)

In a POE the children are asked to predict what will happen in a certain situation. They then describe what actually happens. Following this they try to explain what they have observed. Sometimes the children's observations will take them by surprise and force them to reconsider their ideas.

Examples of POEs could be:

(a) The water from a short fat container is to be poured into a tall thin container and the children are asked to predict the water level.

(b) A sunken soft drinks can is to be filled with air using a plastic tube and the children are asked to predict what will happen to the can.

Can you identify an aspect of science that you will be teaching soon where you could elicit ideas using this technique?

**Activity 5 – Concept Mapping**
(Time required: 1–2 hours)
Concept mapping involves children selecting and noting concepts (usually words) and making connections between related ideas. This is usually done by joining the concepts with arrows or lines. The child is then asked to write words on the line to articulate the relationship between the concepts (see an example in Chapter 9).

There are variations on the use of concept maps including using them as a valuable assessment tool (see Willson and Willson, 1994). Teachers need to consider carefully the practical implications of using them with children, such as the children's written language skills. Useful guidance is given by White and Gunstone (1992).

Some teachers have discovered that the children may change their ideas as they complete the concept map! This perceived 'problem' can prove helpful in developing children's ideas. Here we suggest that you organise the production of concept maps with a group. Group concept maps can lead to interesting discussion. This will give you a feel for the children's understanding of the concept. Working as a group in this way is more likely to lead to progression in children's understanding.

**Activity 6 – Concept cartoons**
In this approach, cartoon style drawings are used to present children with alternative viewpoints relating to everyday situations. The ideas in the drawings are based on ideas which are commonly held about the situations as identified through research and teaching. The children are asked to say what they think and to suggest ways of investigating the ideas where appropriate. The drawings tend to generate instant discussion about the particular ideas involved. Children who are normally reluctant to put forward their own ideas will often be able to associate with one of the ideas being expressed in the drawing. During the process of discussion and investigation ideas are often modified. The challenge to the ideas expressed comes from a range of sources including evidence from investigations, views aired in discussions, challenges from the teacher and from the

alternative views expressed in the drawings themselves. An example is shown in Figure 5.3.

Fig. 5.3. An example of a concept cartoon
(from Keogh and Naylor, 1997)

## Other approaches
The strategies discussed above are illustrations of how to take children's ideas into account in ways that are manageable and relevant. Within your own teaching there may be other similar approaches which help your children's ideas to progress. White and Gunstone (1992) are a source of other useful strategies.

## Reviewing practice about eliciting and developing children's ideas
If you have not tried any of the above approaches in your science teaching, consider building one into your planning so that you can evaluate its effectiveness. If a colleague is also prepared to use the same strategy it will assist you both to compare experiences and outcomes. In order to evaluate an approach it will be helpful to note

instances when you were aware of children's ideas being made explicit, opportunities which arose to challenge ideas and any changes in ideas which occurred.

Which approaches can you identify in your own teaching that enable you and your children to be aware of their ideas and which also enable those ideas to be challenged? Do other colleagues use such approaches in their science teaching? Are some approaches more relevant for particular science activities? How can you build these strategies into your planning and the school's overall planning? As an individual or as a whole staff it is worthwhile building up a resource bank of these strategies. It is also helpful to identify these approaches within the whole-school documentation for science.

## DIFFERENTIATION

In recent years there has been an expectation that teachers will emphasise differentiation in their planning. With limited guidance available to support this requirement some teachers feel that meeting this expectation requires considerable additional work. However, observation of many teachers working with their children frequently reveals that they already use a range of differentiation strategies in their teaching.

The view that differentiation is only important for children with special needs is unhelpful. Differentiated approaches are important in helping all children to learn. In all classes there can be children of similar ability who will have different preferred learning styles and who will learn more effectively from different teaching approaches.

If differentiation is important for all children it is essential that a realistic approach is adopted. It is unlikely that teachers will be able to provide differentiated experiences for all of the children all of the time. What is important is that approaches are used which maximise the opportunities for differentiation without placing an unreasonable demand on the teacher. Some of the general strategies which will be helpful have been outlined in the previous chapter. Some of the specific approaches which can be used to support learning by making differentiation manageable are listed below.

### Differentiation strategies
Some authors identify two approaches to differentiation – differentiation by task and differentiation by outcome. This presents an over-simplified view of how differentiation might be achieved. By

identifying only these two approaches an important aspect of differentiation for most teachers is overlooked. Experience reveals that much effective differentiation occurs through the response of the teacher to the children while they are working. During this time teachers relate their learning objectives to what is actually occurring and make adjustments to the expectations demanded of various children.

The teaching strategies listed below can be used at the planning stage to provide experiences which are suitably differentiated. Their use is equally important as the lesson progresses. It is not intended that all the strategies will be employed at one time, rather that the most useful approaches for a particular lesson are identified. The list is not exhaustive. We hope that you will be able to add to it during your reflections on differentiation:

- using a range of approaches to learning;

- building on children's ideas;

- adjusting the level of demand during the activity;

- adjusting the level of scientific skills required;

- varying the distribution of teacher time;

- varying the amount and nature of teacher intervention;

- varying the degree of independence expected of children;

- careful use of questioning;

- varying the response expected;

- varying the pace of learning;

- varying the method of presentation;

- varying the method of recording;

- adjusting the level of linguistic demand;

- adjusting the level of mathematical demand;

- providing a range of resources.

These strategies are discussed in more detail in Book 1 (Bk. 1, Naylor and Keogh, 5).

**Activity 7 – Reviewing practice about differentiation strategies**
*7a – How do you differentiate in science presently?*
Consider a science activity which you have recently taught or which you are about to teach. Using the above list, decide which would be the most appropriate strategies to use for that activity. How would you adjust the level of demand within the activity? For example, if young children were testing whether fabrics were waterproof you might notice that some children have quickly and effectively tested their fabrics and completed the simple tick chart which you have given the children to complete. If you feel that these children have not been sufficiently challenged by the activity you might decide to adjust the level of demand by varying the method of recording and ask them to complete a different chart in which they draw or describe what they have observed happening to the water and the fabric. Alternatively you might decide that, for some children, the tick chart creates too great a demand and you might ask the children to place the fabric in two hoops before helping them to create with you a visual record of their findings.

*7b – Strategies you might use more frequently*
Consider the list of strategies in relation to your current teaching. Which of the strategies are you aware of using regularly in your teaching? Are there some which you use in other curriculum areas which could also be used in science? In what way do you use the strategies? For example, do you use them in planning activities or when you are working with children? Do you use particular strategies with some children and not with others? Could you extend the use of the strategies with which you are familiar to more children or in more situations?

*7c – Trying a new strategy*
Which of the above strategies have you never or hardly ever used? Unless you have a very specific reason for not using a particular strategy, try building one into your planning and/or your work with the children. Evaluate it in terms of ease of use and whether it appears to help to extend or support learning.

*7d – Discuss differentiation*
Work with a colleague to review the strategies which you are each using in your planning and teaching. Ideally this should be through observation of each other's teaching because it is often possible for one person to identify approaches which are being used intuitively by

another. Failing this, share ideas about lessons which you have both taught using the above list to give a focus to the discussion.

### 7e – Making differentiation explicit

Often the issue about differentiation in a school is not that it is not occurring but that it is not made explicit in the planning of lessons and during teaching. One useful approach is to give each strategy which you use in your school a code letter or abbreviation. This allows the main differentiation strategies to be employed in a lesson to be easily identified in planning. It also means that where differentiation is more likely to occur while the children are working it is possible to show that you have anticipated the main approach in advance of the lesson.

### Taking time to reflect

After these activities or indeed any science lesson, a few moments of careful reflection will assist future decisions about strategies you have used. Reflection will help you to decide which strategies are the most effective and the most manageable in your situation.

### A whole-school approach

Any or all of the above review activities could be used at a whole-school level to raise the awareness of differentiation within the school. Ultimately a whole-school approach will be the most effective way of working to support children's learning. As a staff it will be helpful to decide which are the strategies which you wish to use within your teaching. These can then be described in detail and included in the school's policies. This should lead to a more systematic and explicit use of the strategies, providing greater consistency throughout the school and enabling new staff to use those approaches which are seen as appropriate by the school. It should also mean that suitable resources which take into account the need for differentiation can be developed or acquired and be made available to the whole staff.

### BIBLIOGRAPHY

Department for Education and the Welsh Office (1995) *Science in the National Curriculum*, London: HMSO.

Jarman, R., Keogh, B. and Naylor, S. (1994) *I've Done This Before: Continuity and Progression in School Science*, Hatfield: Association for Science Education.

Keogh, B. and Naylor, S. (1997) *Starting Points for Science*, Sandbach: Millgate House.

White, R. and Gunstone, R. (1992) *Probing Understanding*, London: Falmer Press.

Willson, S. and Willson, M. (1994) Concept mapping as an assessment tool, *Primary Science Review*, no. 34, pp. 14–16.

# 6
# Equal Opportunities

*Gill Peet*

## INTRODUCTION

The greatest problem facing co-ordinators or initial teacher trainers trying to encourage teachers or student teachers to think about questions of equality in their teaching is to establish recognition that there is an issue to be dealt with. Resistance can be even greater in science because there is a widespread view that science is neutral and culture free (Bk. 1, Peet, 6).

The series of activities outlined below are in three stages. The first stage activities are for the co-ordinator to use with staff and are designed to try and overcome this resistance by helping teachers to recognise that we all have prejudices and to admit that these prejudices can work to the disadvantage of others. (Subsequent activities can be completed either in groups or by teachers working on their own.) The second stage activities are designed to help teachers recognise that science is not culture free and to appreciate the role that science can play in eradicating prejudice. The final stage considers classroom strategies that give equality of opportunity to all our pupils and at the same time work against prejudices being developed in those we teach. The activities are intended to challenge teachers to examine their own views on our multicultural society in which we purport to give equality of opportunity regardless of race, gender, socio-economic class or disability or any other identifiable group; then to consider the implications for their practice in the classroom especially in their science teaching. The aim is to ensure that no child in the primary school is disadvantaged at an early age from later either pursuing a career in science and technology or from using science as part of their lives in work or as citizens.

Activities are not designed to be necessarily worked through systematically but can be dipped into according to the needs of the group. Because of this some activities have similar objectives.

## STAGE ONE: RECOGNISING THE ISSUE

In Book 1 I argued that prejudice is widespread and is the fundamental cause of inequality in our society. It is claimed that inequality of opportunity results from prejudice that 'operates through a common process of stereotyping and devaluation which has the effect of legitimising discrimination against specific groups and thus maintaining the advantages of the majority by limiting the opportunities of the specific group or groups being discriminated against' (Bk. 1, Peet, 6).

Most teachers would be horrified to think that their teaching did not give equality of opportunity to all the children in their class and would argue that they treat all children the same. Nevertheless, prejudice was claimed by Lord Swann (1985) as being the root of the problems of under-achievement by ethnic minority children in schools.

**Activity 1 – Recognising that we all have stereotyped images**
(Time required: about 30 minutes)
Ask teachers either individually or in pairs to draw a scientist.

It is likely that stereotyped images of bearded, balding, eccentric-looking men in white lab coats will be portrayed. This is a short exercise that both breaks the ice and can be a good starting point for discussion. Teachers can be encouraged to develop their discussion into their own feelings about science. It may be that somebody will admit that they were put off science by 'the image'.

Considerable research has been done into children's perception of a scientist and research still indicates that scientists are seen as men, balding with beards, wearing glasses and white lab coats and making potions. Figure 6.1 includes examples drawn by PGCE (Primary) teacher education students at the start of their course. Figure 6.2 shows an analysis of the pictures drawn by sixteen children. Teachers could try the exercise with the children in their own classes.

Historically there has always been a low uptake of physical sciences and engineering amongst girls. Most of the girls who do take up science opt for life sciences. There is a view that this is somehow more suitable for a girl. Research has shown that even at an early age children stereotype according to gender. In research done by Alan Smithers and Pauline Zientek when children were asked to indicate whether

Fig. 6.1. Images of scientists drawn by teacher education students

Fig. 6.1. Images of scientists drawn by teacher education students (*cont*)

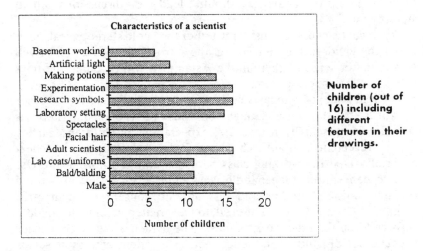

Fig. 6.2. Analysis of pictures of scientists drawn by children
(from *Images of Scientists* by Mark Preston (1995))

pictures of certain activities were suitable only for boys, girls or both sexes, both boys and girls saw 'scientist' as a predominantly male occupation (Smithers and Zientek, 1991)

## Activity 2 – Recognising that we all hold stereotypical images
(Time required: 30 minutes)
The aims of this activity are the same as for Activity 1.

If possible, split into groups of no more than four. The aim is to allow discussion but be in small enough groups for everybody to take part.

Give the groups a set of photographs showing faces. These should be taken from newspapers or be of people you know who have a range of occupations. Try to avoid stereotypical images.

The task is to match the careers to the pictures. If people try to play the game by deliberately choosing people who look unlikely, it can be pointed out that that in itself is recognising stereotyping.

When the task is complete the real information is revealed about each person.

## The effect of stereotypical views on teaching

Both the above activities should lead to discussions about stereotyping.

Try to get teachers to consider whether they hold stereotypical views about the children they teach, e.g. the Afro-Caribbean children will have a better sense of rhythm; the Asian girls will be quiet; the boys will be better at science, etc.

The real issue, of course, is not that stereotyping exists but whether it works to the disadvantage of those stereotyped. There is considerable research on teachers' expectations of children. Hartley (1978) researched infant school pupils and found that teachers generally rated the working class pupils as untidier, noisier and less able to concentrate than middle class pupils. Boys were also rated rougher, noisier, untidier and less able to concentrate than girls. Gender differences were believed to be greater among the middle class children than the working class. The evidence that such teacher expectations of children influence their interactions with them seems to indicate that boys are given more help than girls and are reprimanded more frequently (Bossert, 1983; Lindow, Marrett and Wilkinson, 1985; Brophy, 1985; Mortimore et al, 1988). Brophy and Good (1974) showed that teachers gave the pupils they believed to be clever longer to answer teacher questions, and gave them more prompts and hints than they gave pupils who were believed to be stupid.

## STAGE TWO: LOOKING AT SCIENCE AND EQUAL OPPORTUNITIES

There is a view that prejudice is only an issue for the inner city multi-ethnic school. However, prejudice is as much, if not more, the concern of the so-called middle class 'all white' school and is in some respects even more fundamental because we need to be aware of the prejudices that are being developed by the children we are teaching. We need to be aware of the insidious effect of stereotyping and the prejudice that develops from it.

In order to ensure that we provide equality of opportunity in our science teaching and that our teaching works to elimimate prejudice, we need to consider our views of science and the science we teach.

### Activity 3 – To raise awareness of the nature of science

(Time required: 30 minutes)
This can be done individually but for best advantage is best done in

Pupils should be educated about people who are different from themselves.

Science is the same in every country.

It is necessary to teach science from other countries in order to develop an equal society.

Equality of opportunity is not a problem in our school because we don't have any ethnic minority children or children from disadvantaged homes and we treat boys and girls alike.

It is difficult to change the way we teach because of the National Curriculum.

I don't know enough about cultures other than my own to be able to adapt my teaching style.

Teaching can reinforce existing prejudices.

Fig. 6.3. Statements for Activity 3

| the compass | sunspots | gunpowder |
| --- | --- | --- |

| magnetic remanance – (the magnetic induction that remains in a material after removal of the magnetising force) |
| --- |

| cast iron | the crank handle | paper |
| --- | --- | --- |

| deep drilling for natural gas | the suspension bridge | the fishing reel |
| --- | --- | --- |

| underwater salvage operations | biological pest control | matches |
| --- | --- | --- |

| the wheelbarrow | porcelain | the umbrella |
| --- | --- | --- |

| chess | brandy | the parachute |
| --- | --- | --- |

| whisky | paper money | endocrinology |
| --- | --- | --- |

| printing | the spinning wheel | the decimal system |
| --- | --- | --- |

| diabetes | the kite | the crossbow |
| --- | --- | --- |

| the mechanical clock | chemical warfare |
| --- | --- |

Fig. 6.4. List of inventions and discoveries for Activity 4
(from Temple, R. (1991) published in Reiss, M. J. (1993) *Science Education for a Pluralist Society*, Buckingham: Open University Press)

groups of two to four where views can be exchanged and ideas challenged.

Photocopy the statements in Figure 6.3 and cut them out separately. Ask the participants to consider the statements and to place them into piles of agree or disagree. If one group finishes earlier than another they can be asked to put them into a heirarchy. They may need to create a third group of 'don't know'.

When the task is completed discussion should focus on points of doubt in order for teachers to clarify their own views.

### Activity 4 – To recognise the Eurocentricity of the science we teach

(Time required: 30 minutes)

Photocopy the list of inventions and discoveries in Figure 6.4 and cut them up into individual inventions. After discussion with colleagues put them into piles according to which country you feel was the first to discover them. It would not be productive to spend too much time on this activity and you may decide that it would be preferable to simply have one pile of European discoveries and one for non-European.

In fact everything on this list was discovered by the Chinese hundreds of years ago and in some cases thousands of years before they were discovered in the West (Needham, 1954). Through examples such as paper, printing, gunpowder and the compass, Dennick (1992) points out how there has been a tendency to disparage and downgrade the discoveries and achievements of other cultures. Paper and printing were developed in China in the second and eighth centuries AD respectively but printing is usually ascribed to Gutenberg in the fifteenth century. Dennick also points out that although the discovery of gunpowder has been ascribed to Roger Bacon in 1269 AD its use in ninth-century China is well documented. Similarly, William Gilbert is commonly claimed to have discovered the use of the magnet as a compass in the sixteenth century although in fact the Chinese regularly used magnets as a navigational aid in the eleventh century. Even Newton's first law had previously been recognised by the early Chinese.

Dennick also tells us that 'Islamic scientists discovered the pulmonary circulation of the blood, heliocentric theories of the solar system and important ideas in optics which are frequently ascribed to European traditions'.

Other examples of early discoveries can be found in the hieroglyphics on the walls of temples in Egypt such as those at Kom

67

Ombo temple which show that the Egyptians had a high level of surgical knowledge two thousand years ago.

These examples should serve to illustrate that while European science has much to be proud of, it is not unique. Few teachers will have much knowledge of anything other than a Eurocentric view of science and it is a very real problem for them to know how to address the situation. To add the odd fact may be construed as tokenism and may in fact do more harm than good. In order to deal with this aspect effectively there needs to be a real commitment to anti-racist science.

## Activity 5 – Reinforcement of the previous activity: minority groups as scientists

(Time required: 30 minutes)

Teachers should be asked to name as many black, non-European or women scientists as they can.

Hopefully some suggestions can be made and knowledge thus shared. It is likely, however, that many teachers will only know Marie Curie and it will be necessary for you to supplement their knowledge. Book 1 gives the examples of Charles Richard Drew, the inventor of blood banks, and Elijah McCoy, who invented a device for lubricating locomotive engines (the real McCoy), both of whom were black Americans, and Caroline Herschel, the sister of William Herschel and who discovered eight comets herself. Other examples are shown in Figure 6.5.

---

The following list of black, non-European and women scientists is taken with permission from a much more extensive and informative list in *Science Education for a Pluralist Society* by Michael J. Reiss (1993, Open University Press)

**Ibn Nafis** was an Islamic scientist who died in 1288 and who discovered pulmonary circulation.

**Mrs Hutton** was a botanist and pharmacist in the eighteenth century who discovered that extracts from foxgloves could be used to treat heart disease. She sold her recipe to Dr William Withering who is usually accredited with the discovery of digitalis.

**Davidson Nicol** was born in 1924. Because he was black he was not allowed to become a cardiologist in London. He eventually worked out the chemical structure of insulin.

---

**Dorothy Hodgkin** was born in Cairo in 1910. Her work led to a better understanding of penicillin, vitamin B12 and insulin. When she received the Nobel Prize in 1964 one tabloid paper used the headline 'Housewife wins Nobel Prize'. She was recognised in 1996 when her picture was put on a 20p stamp.

**Garret Morgan** was an Afro-American who invented the gas mask.

**Ida Tacke Noddack** was born in 1896. She discovered thenium and was the first person to suggest the existence of nuclear fission.

**Lewis Howard Latimer** (1848–1928) was an Afro-American scientist born six years after his father had fled from slavery. He refined Edison's light bulb so that instead of only burning for a week it would burn for months.

**Chang Heng** (78–139) was a Chinese astronomer who recognised that the source of the moon's light was sunlight and that lunar eclipses were caused by the Earth's shadow falling upon it.

**Ibn al-Haitham** (c. 965–1038) was an Egyptian Islamic scholar generally known in the West as Alhazen. He rejected the view that light was emitted by the eye and instead claimed that it was emitted from self-luminous sources and was reflected and refracted and perceived by the eye.

Fig. 6.5. Examples of black, non-European and women scientists

It might be useful during this stage to show as overheads or use as handouts the quotations in Figure 6.6 which indicate why we should be considering adding a multicultural dimension to our science teaching.

'Because science is a human activity, scientific ideas are developed in a cultural and a socio-political context and must be influenced by the values and institutions of that culture. Science and scientists are therefore not neutral. It is important to recognise that different societies have viewed science in different ways. It is important that science is taught in its human, social, cultural and environmental contexts, and there are related issues which cannot be ignored if science education is to be a positive force in tackling racism and raising children's awareness.'
(ASE (1989) *Multicultural Education Working Party Discussion Paper*, Hatfield, Herts: Association for Science Education, p. 2)

'People from all cultures are involved in scientific enterprise. The curriculum should reflect the contributions from different cultures, for example, the origins and growth of chemistry from ancient Egypt, Greece and Arabia to the later Byzantine and European cultures, and parallel developments in China and India. It is important that science books and other learning materials should include examples of people from ethnic minority groups working alongside others and achieving success in scientific work. Pupils should come to realise the international nature of science and the potential it has for helping to overcome racial prejudice.'
(DES (1995) *Science in the National Curriculum*, Department of Education and Science and the Welsh Office, London: HMSO, A10, 7.8)

Fig. 6.6. Why we need a multicultural dimension to our science teaching

## STAGE THREE: PLANNING TO ELIMINATE STEREOTYPING IN SCIENCE ACTIVITIES AND PROMOTE EQUALITY

Research has shown that children's attitudes differ according to whether other cultures are portrayed favourably or unfavourably in books (Zimet, 1976; Campbell and Wirtenberg, 1980).

### Activity 6 – Looking for stereotyping in books
(Time required: 1 hour)
Gather a selection of photocopied pages from a wide range of primary science textbooks. In groups analyse them according to the following questions:

1. Do the pictures provide strong role models with whom ethnic minority children can identify?

2. Are the activities and illustrations presented in a manner that will discourage feelings of superiority in any group of children, e.g. European or boys?

3. Are the illustrations stereotypical?

4. Are women positively represented?

5. Is the language content free of insulting and degrading language?

6. Is the language accessible to children from all backgrounds?

7. Are the activities culturally specific?

8. What image of science is portrayed? For example, is sound portrayed through the use of western musical instruments?

9. How are boys and girls portrayed? (e.g. boys doing and girls being passive)

10. Are disabled people ever shown?

11. Are the resources appropriate for a variety of pupil needs and abilities?

### Activity 7 – making science accessible
(Time required: 15 minutes)
Give a comprehension activity in a language that is difficult to understand. By changing the everyday words into gobbledegook the passage will be difficult if not impossible to understand. The purpose is to empathise with children who can read but who are not familiar with the meaning of many of the everyday words we use. A translation is provided in the note at the end of this chapter.

*Example*
Take a riter and a braiting trock. Can you make a blee-bloe? Take two identical stronts and put one on each end of the blee-bloe. Does it skattle? Try moving the trock nearer to one end and putting the stronts on the ends. Does it skattle now? Keep changing the position of the trock. Does it have to be in the sindel to skattle?
(Adapted from a passage in *Collins Primary Science – Nursery Rhymes*, p. 29)

### Activity 8 – Organising our classrooms to ensure equality of access for all
(Time required: 2 hours+)
Look at the following checklist and consider whether your classroom has these characteristics:

| National Curriculum | Activity | Opportunity for multicultural content | Avoiding prejudice and stereotyping |
|---|---|---|---|
| | Looking a wide range of clothes | Ensure that clothes from other cultures are included. Name them using appropriate language to describe the clothes | Encourage respect of difference by discussing reasons why clothes are different, e.g. religion, climate, etc. |
| Sc. 1 PoS 1, 2, 3 | Investigation into the most suitable colour for wearing to stay cool | Looking at why white is often worn in hot countries | Respecting and valuing judgements of others |
| | Investigation into the best material for keeping warm | Thinking about the use of animal skins in cold countries. | Accepting that we also use leather for clothes |

Fig. 6.7. Key Stage 1 topic on clothes
(from Bk. 1, Peet, 6)

1. Is it welcoming to all children? Are there children who do not mix? Are there children who have difficulty understanding English? Do the children of different gender, from different social classes or cultures mix with each other in group work and socially?

2. How much do the children know about each other's cultures? How much do you know about their culture?

3. Do the children learn about science from cultures that are both their own and different from their own?

4. Do all children take an equal part in science activities regardless of gender, class or culture or do some children take a more active part than others?

5. Do you have a variety of resources in the classroom that can add an equal opportunities dimension to a science activity. For

72

example, male or ethnic dolls that can be used to represent people in investigations, e.g. when finding the best material to keep the doll dry, etc.

6. Do you have appropriate expectations of all children regardless of gender, class or culture?

### Activity 9 – Planning activities to eliminate prejudice
(Time required: 50 minutes+)
Use a grid like the one in Figure 6.7 and try and plan activities that will involve a multicultural, class dimension and that will take the opportunity to discourage prejudice through stereotyping.

## CONCLUSION

It is only through recognising that there is an issue to be dealt with and accepting that science is not culture free that we can begin to work towards providing equality of opportunity in science for all our children regardless of their background. It is therefore more important that we convey that message than that we create complicated planning sheets which teachers do not understand and ultimately will not use.

*Note*:
Translation of gobbledegook text in Activity 7:

> Take a ruler and a building block. Can you make a see-saw? Take two identical weights and put one at each end of the see-saw. Does it balance? Try moving the building block nearer to one end and putting the weights on the ends. Does it balance now? Keep changing the position of the block. Does it have to be in the middle to balance?
>
> (Howe, 1990)

## BIBLIOGRAPHY

ASE (1989) *Multicultural Education Working Party Discussion Paper*, Hatfield, Herts: Association for Science Education.

Bossert, S. (1983) Understanding sex differences in children's classroom experience, in W. Doyle and E. Good (eds) *Focus on Teaching*, Chicago: The University Press.

Brophy, J. (1985) Interactions of male and female students with male and female teachers, in L. Wilkinson and C. B. Marrett (eds) *Gender Influences in Classroom Interaction*, Orlando, FL: Academic Press.

Brophy, J. E. and Good, T. L. (1974) *Teacher–Student Relationships*, New York: Holt Rinehart & Winston.

Campbell, B. and Wirtenberg, J. (1980) How books influence children: what the research shows, *Interracial Books for Children Bulletin*, Vol. 11, no. 6.

Dennick, R. (1992) *Multicultural and Antiracist Science Education: Theory and Practice*, School of Education, University of Nottingham.

DES (1995) *Science in the National Curriculum*, Department of Education and Science and the Welsh Office, London: HMSO.

Hartley, D. (1978) Sex and social class: a case study of an infant school, *British Educational Research Journal*, Vol. 4, no. 2.

Howe, L. (1990) *Collins Primary Science Key Stage 1, Set One; Nursery Rhymes*, London: Collins Educational.

Lindow, J., Marrett, C. B. and Wilkinson, L. C. (1985) Overview, in L. C. Wilkinson and C. B. Marrett (eds) *Gender Influences in Classroom Interaction*, Orlando, FL: Academic Press.

Mortimore, P., Sammons, P., Stoll, L., Lewis, D. and Ecob, R. (1988) *School Matters*, Wells, Somerset: Open Books.

Needham, J. (1954) *Science and Civilisation in China*, Cambridge University Press.

Peet, G. (1996) Equal opportunities and the teaching of science, in *Teaching Science in the Primary School, Book 1*, Plymouth: Northcote House.

Preston, Mark (1995) Images of scientists, *Primary Science Review*, no. 37, April.

Reiss, M. J. (1993) *Science Education for a Pluralist Society*, Buckingham: Open University Press.

Smithers, A. and Zientek, P. (1991) *Gender, Primary Schools and the National Curriculum*, NASUWT and The Engineering Council.

Swann Report (1985) *Education for All; The Report of the Committee of Inquiry into the Education of Children from Ethnic Minority Groups*, Cmnd. 9453, London: HMSO.

Zimet, S. G. (1976) *Print and Prejudice*, London: Hodder and Stoughton.

# 7
# Science in the Early Years

*Karen Hartley and Christine Macro*

## INTRODUCTION

In this chapter we deal with a number of questions that we have identified through our work with teachers and students. We have previously discussed the challenges that face teachers of young children as they plan and implement the science curriculum (Bk. 1, Hartley and Macro, 7). There is, we feel, a consensus that there is a need to begin children's learning about the phenomena of the world at an early age; that in a very natural way, the young child's innate inquisitiveness can be channelled effectively in science activities. We are aware that for teachers this involves identifying elements of science in the diverse early years curriculum and planning teaching and learning situations carefully. In this chapter we have suggested tasks which will help teachers and students to reflect upon these challenges and to examine ways in which they might be met. Whilst we acknowledge that some teachers might wish to explore these issues in their own classroom, there is nevertheless a need for a shared understanding and some of our activities would be better developed in a whole-school context in order to encourage further development of quality in all children's learning.

## HOW MUCH SCIENCE KNOWLEDGE DO TEACHERS NEED TO TEACH SCIENCE EFFECTIVELY?

This question has recently been the subject of debate. Although the view is not universally held, there are those who feel that teacher confidence is related to scientific understanding and that the teacher who has a firm grasp of key concepts is able to teach more effectively.

Harlen, Holroyd and Byrne (1995) discussed this issue when reporting on the study carried out for the Scottish Council for Research in Education. They found that, although it would be a mistake to assume that 'confidence and understanding always go together [nevertheless] often they do'. They were able to show that low confidence had several effects such as teaching little science, relying on prescriptive texts and workcards and over-reliance on expository techniques. Alexander, Rose and Woodhead (1992) stated that subject knowledge was critical 'at every point in the teaching process: in planning, assessing and diagnosing, task setting, questioning, explaining and giving feedback.' Feasey (1994) confirmed that some teachers were reluctant to place themselves in a position where their own inadequate personal knowledge would be revealed. In Book 1 we argued that before teachers can plan the work for the children in the early years there is a need for them to identify the key ideas in the topics the classes are to study and to explore their own understanding of these ideas. Shulman (1987) suggests that teaching involves an 'exchange of ideas' and that 'exemplary teachers present ideas in order to provoke the constructive processes of their students.'

The tasks that follow might help you to consider your own scientific knowledge and to reflect on ways in which you and other teachers can help each other.

## Activity 1 – Preparing an audit and action plan
(Time required: 1 hour)
If we accept the current view that subject knowledge is important, we should consider how it can help us to be more effective in our teaching (Bk. 1, Hartley and Macro, 7). Teachers who have a sound subject knowledge are in a better position to:

- provide appropriate experiences;
- develop key ideas;
- ask pertinent questions;
- encourage children to see links between experiences;
- give accurate explanations and use analogies which will be relevant to the children;
- help pupils to make relevant observations when looking for evidence;
- know where to go next in terms of children's learning of a concept;

● reflect the role of science in society and everyday life.

Consider where you are, individually, and as a staff, in terms of your subject knowledge.

What can you/your school do to improve on this position?

Suggest three or four ways in which teachers could help each other to become more confident in addressing the issues. Collect these ideas and prioritise them. It is important that you inform the school's senior management about the results. You should negotiate about when and how the needs for science subject knowledge might be included in the school development plan.

Define what action needs to be taken and set up realistic target dates for the implementation of the strategies.

## Activity 2 – Sharing ideas about forces
(Time required: 1 hour)
In this activity you will use material taken from *Knowledge and*

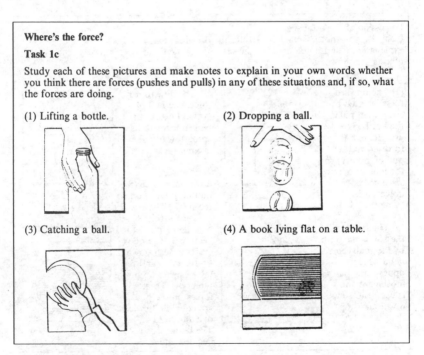

**Where's the force?**

**Task 1c**

Study each of these pictures and make notes to explain in your own words whether you think there are forces (pushes and pulls) in any of these situations and, if so, what the forces are doing.

(1) Lifting a bottle.

(2) Dropping a ball.

(3) Catching a ball.

(4) A book lying flat on a table.

Fig. 7.1. Finding out about forces (Activity 2)
(from NCC, 1992)

*Understanding of Science: Forces – A Guide for Teachers* (NCC, 1992). This activity could form the basis of a session with colleagues even though the book does enable teachers to examine their own subject knowledge and to work on their own. The book suggested is one of a series and was free to schools. (For addresses and details of other titles see the Bibliography.)

Look at the section reproduced in Figure 7.1. Make notes about your ideas and about any questions which you would like to ask. Use the questions as a focus for discussion. Here are some to get you started:

- How many definitions of force have been generated?

- What do you feel about the scientists' views? (Fig. 7.2)

- What happens when you squash a piece of foam rubber or sponge?

- What can you see?

---

**Discussion of Tasks 1c and 1d**
Compare your notes from Task 1c and the drawings made in Task 1d with these explanations. Please note that for the sake of simplicity not all the forces acting on the objects are shown.

(1) The upward force, exerted by the person pulling the bottle, is greater than the force down (the pull of gravity) so the milk bottle starts to move downwards.

(2) The downward force (the pull of gravity) causes the ball to increase its speed towards the ground.

4) There is a downward force (the pull of gravity) on the book. The reason for this is considered further in Section 3. The book exerts a push down on the table and the table pushes up on the book. These forces on the book are equal and cancel one another out. The book does not begin to move.

(3) The force on the ball is the push by the goalkeeper's hand which opposes the ball's movement and causes it to slow down and stop.

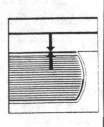

Fig. 7.2. The scientists' views (Activity 2)
(from NCC, 1992)

- How does your knowledge of balanced forces help you to explain what you notice?

If you are using this task as a staff development activity, do it in pairs, then in fours and later with the whole staff in order to ensure that you have a shared understanding.

## HOW CAN WE ENSURE THAT OUR PROVISION FOR CHILDREN IN THE EARLY YEARS IS APPROPRIATE?

The following activities provide opportunities to reflect on how simple everyday materials can be used in the three stages: **exploration, guided investigation and independent investigation.** Figure 7.3 is taken from Book 1 and you might also like to read a further consideration of progression (Bk. 1, Naylor and Keogh, 4).

| *Experiences* | *Potential learning* |
|---|---|
| **Early exploration** | |
| Children help the teacher to mix orange juice with water to make ice lollies by putting sticks into the tray and placing it in the freezer. | Teacher helps the children to notice how the liquid changes colour when water is added and how the sticks can move in the liquid. Children may observe that the liquid takes the shape of the container. |
| Lollies are taken out of the freezer. Children lick them and feel them. | Children are encouraged to talk about what they notice. The lollies are now **hard** and the stick is held **firm** by the **frozen** liquid (ice). As the children lick the lollies they feel **cold** and begin to **soften**. Some children may talk about the air or their warm mouths changing the shape and the texture of the ice. |
| One lolly is put back into a freezer bag. This is compared after a few minutes with those which are exposed to warm mouths. | Children may talk about what they notice. If a lolly is left in the freezer bag it stays hard and cold. |
| One lolly is left in the room on a saucer. | A lolly left in the room changes back to a liquid. |

**Guided investigation**

Teacher talks with and questions children about 'What will happen if we leave a lolly in the warm classroom?'

A lolly may melt in the warm classroom.

What might happen if we leave a lolly in a fridge and another in a freezer bag?

The lolly in the fridge may melt slowly. The lolly in the freezer bag will stay solid.

Teacher and children together plan a fair test to find out in what conditions the lollies melt: 1 lolly in a fridge, 1 lolly in a freezer bag, 1 lolly in a warm room.

Children are given opportunities to suggest what might happen (to predict).

Teacher talks to children about how to keep the test fair: e.g. (a) same mixture of orange and water (b) same size and shape of lolly (c) when lollies are frozen hard leave them in the fridge, freezer bag and room for the same length of time.

Children may recognise when a test is fair. Children talk about and try to give explanations about what they notice.

Observe and discuss results.

Present results by drawing, writing or using teacher-designed tables.

**Independent investigation**

Children look at lollies of different shapes and are encouraged to raise questions, e.g. does a short, wide lolly melt more quickly than a long, thin lolly?

Turning ideas into a form which can be investigated. Thinking about what might happen, e.g. 'I think a long, thin lolly will melt more quickly than a short, wide lolly.'

Children plan what to do in order to answer the question. eg What might they use as jelly moulds? How long to leave in the freezer? What variables should they keep the same (e.g. same amount of liquid)?

Planning what to do. Making measurements. Children measure liquids and record time left in the freezer, fridge and room.

How to decide which melts most quickly.

Recording observations by writing and drawing. For example, after 3, 5 and 10 minutes. Using results to draw conclusions. Providing explanations.

Fig. 7.3. Progression in early years science
(Bk. 1, Hartley and Macro, 7, pp. 98–9)

## Activity 3 – Defining exploration
(Time required: 15–20 minutes)
In Book 1 we discussed how children might move from:

**Early exploration**
to
**Guided investigation**
to
**Independent investigation**

Work with a selection or all of the following materials:

● coloured liquids;

● a collection of flowers;

● fruits to make a fruit salad;

● a collection of bubble mixtures, wands and blowers.

Use your materials for **exploration**. Play with them and note down any aspects of learning in science which you might consider significant. What might be the intentions for learning in a lesson plan?

## Activity 4 – Identifying guided investigation
(Time required: 15–20 minutes)
Use the same materials and think about some questions for investigation. Consider how you might help children who were engaged in **Guided investigation**. What might be the intentions for learning in a lesson plan?

## Activity 5 – Identifying independent investigation
(Time required: 15–20 minutes)
If you were to use the same materials in order to develop the skills of **Independent investigation**, how would you proceed? Identify the learning intentions in the lesson or lessons.

You might like to use Figure 7.3 as an example and produce something similar for each context (coloured liquids, collections, fruits and bubbles).

## HOW IMPORTANT ARE THE WORDS? HOW CAN WE GET THE CHILDREN TO THINK?

We have suggested that encouraging children to think is important in their learning (Bk. 1, Hartley and Macro, 7). A further exploration of the ways in which children formulate ideas appears in Book 1 (McGuigan and Schilling, 2, and Heywood, 3).

Extending children's thinking could be done through teachers commenting on the children's observations, questioning their ideas and enabling the children to relate one experience to another. A writer who addresses the issue of teachers' questions is Elstgeest (1985).

The next activity will enable you to think about how your questions might help children to develop science skills and scientific ideas.

### Activity 6 – Framing questions
(Time required: 30 minutes)
Look at the photographs in Figure 7.4. What questions could be asked to encourage the children's thinking about scientific phenomena?

You may like to use a proforma such as the one outlined below.

| Questions | Potential for developing ideas | Potential for developing appropriate elements of science |
|---|---|---|
|  |  |  |

Fig.7.4.

Fig.7.4.

## Activity 7 – Providing a variety of contexts
(Time required: 1 hour)
Consider this case study:

> In his long-term planning, an infant teacher identified the need for the
> children in his Year 1 class to experience changes of state. He wanted to
> do this at different times of the year and using a variety of contexts. The
> web in Figure 7.5 shows the range of experiences that children might have
> during the year in order to develop the understanding that in order for
> melting to take place a source of heat is required. As well as exploring
> the melting process he would also help children to recognise that when
> a melting substance is cooled it may not look the same as at the outset
> (e.g. ice cream) but that no new substance has formed as it has melted.

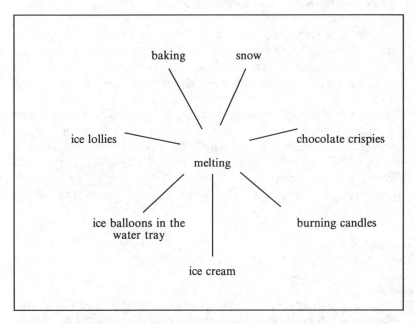

Fig. 7.5. Real life contexts which include examples of melting

Using the web as a focus, discuss the following:

● When would be an appropriate time during the year to introduce
   activities related to these resources? Would you use them in more
   than one context?

- Identify the potential for learning within each experience. What key ideas could be developed?

- What would be the focus of the discussions within each experience? What language would you wish to encourage?

- How would the experiences be linked to each other? Can you identify useful analogies or 'memory joggers' for the children?

- Select one of the following and identify experiences that could be undertaken at different times of the year to develop understanding of the key concepts involved:

**pushes/pulls**      **air**      **habitats**      **sound**

## Activity 8 – Finding out children's ideas
(Time required: 30 minutes)
As a stimulus for introducing work on friction, a teacher read the story 'Wheels' (Graham, 1986) to a group of nursery children. Over the following days she joined in the children's play with cars on a selection of different surfaces before talking to them individually to find out their ideas.

Consider the transcripts below and identify the children's ideas and the strategies used by the teacher in finding out their thinking. Suggest responses that you might have made in this situation to develop their thinking about friction. What might the children say that would indicate their understanding?

How might the strategies and responses be different if the activity were to be undertaken with children in Year 1 or 2?

### Transcripts
T = Teacher  C = *Child*

### Matthew
T  Can you remember in our story where the little boy didn't like riding his bike?
C  *In the mud.*
T  And why didn't he like riding in the mud?
C  *Because his wheels sank in.*
T  Then what couldn't he do?
C  *He couldn't pedal.*
T  He couldn't, that's right. Where else did he not like riding his bike?
C  *In the puddle.*

T  Why?

C  *Because he was getting all wet.*

T  And where else did he not like riding?

C  *In the grass.*

T  Why not?

C  *Because his wheels sunk in and he couldn't get . . . pedal.*

T  There was one more place he didn't like riding his bike.

C  *The kitchen floor.*

T  Shall we have a look in the book (look in the book together). Do you know what this is?

C  *The living room carpet.*

T  Did he like riding on that?

C  *No his wheel sank.*

T  These slopes we have been looking at, can you remember which ones our cars go faster on?

C  *Kitchen floor and wood.*

T  Does it go fast on any other ones?

C  *Plastic.*

T  What about on this one? (sandpaper)

C  *Slow.*

T  What about on the carpet?

C  *Slow.*

T  What about on these stones?

C  *Slow.*

T  Do you know why it goes slowly on the stones?

C  *Because it's all bumpy and rough.*

T  That's right. Do you know why the cars go slowly on the carpet?

C  *Because it's soft.*

T  And what happens to the car?

C  *The wheels sink in.*

T  Why do you think the cars go fast on the wood?

C  *Because they didn't sink in.*

T  And why didn't they sink in?

C  *Because it's hard.*

T  I have three cars here Matthew. One big one and two small ones. What do you think might happen to this one on the stones?

C  (Tries car on the stones) *It won't go.*

T  Why won't it go?

C  *Because it's stuck on the stones.*

T  What happens to this one? (Car goes down the slope)

C  *It moves.*

T  What will happen to this one?

C *It won't move.*
T Do you think that they will all go down the wood?
C *Yes fast.*
T Why do you think that they'll all go down the wood?
C *Because they won't sink.* (tries all cars)
T Do you know how we could make the cars go faster?
C *Make it higher.* (He is referring to the slope)
T If you were to ride your bike on the surfaces which one do you think would be best?
C *Plastic.*
T Thank you Matthew.

## Mary

T Can you remember what happened in the story?
C *All that the boy liked was the kitchen floor.*
T He liked somewhere else. Can you remember?
C *On the path.*
T And do you know why he liked riding on the kitchen floor?
C *Because it was nice and hard.*
T Where did he not like riding his bike?
C *In the puddles and in the mud.*
T Why did he not like them?
C *Because he sinks.*
T When he sunk. What couldn't he do?
C *Ride his bike.*
T I have some slopes here and some cars. Which ones will the cars go fast on?
C *That one and that one* (plastic and wood) *and that one and that one* (carpet and sandpaper).
T Why do you think it will go fast on these?
C *Because it's nice and hard.*
T Is the carpet hard?
C *Yes.*
T Which ones do the cars go slowly on?
C *Stones.*
T And why does it go slowly on the stones?
C *Because it's stones.*
T And what do the stones do?
C *The wheel sinks in.*
T What do you think will happen to this yellow truck on the stones?
C *Go fast.*
T What will happen to these two cars on the stones?

C  *Go slow.* (cars go slowly down the slope)
T  Why do the cars go slowly?
C  *Because it's bumpy.*
T  Which of these surfaces do you think the car will go fast on?
C  *The kitchen floor.*
T  What will happen to all these cars?
C  *Go fast.*
T  Why do they go fast?
C  *Because it's hard.*
T  And is it bumpy or smooth?
C  *Smooth.*
T  Do you know how we could make the cars go faster?
C  *No* (pause). *Push them.*
T  If you wanted to ride your bike which one would be best for you to ride on?
C  *The path.*
T  Would you like to ride on any of these?
C  *The plastic.*
T  Thank you for your help Mary.

(The transcripts are reproduced with the permission of Joanne Boynton.)

You might like to tape-record a small group of children talking or 'interview' individuals and analyse the children's current understanding. What strategies might you use to move the children on in their thinking?

## HOW DO I KNOW THEY ARE LEARNING THROUGH PLAY?

Play is a recognised feature in early years classrooms yet often questions are raised about the value of such activity. Much research has been undertaken into children's learning through play and we have previously mentioned this (Bk. 1, Hartley and Macro, 7). As the focus of a final dissertation in her science course a student observed a group of young children involved in sand play. As a result of her observations she was able to identify the learning outcomes within this situation. Further observations were then carried out to determine how often these learning outcomes occurred. These outcomes are identified in Figure 7.6.

---

**Scientific sand play**

**Planning:** when children discuss with other children what their play is going to be before they start.

**Investigating properties**: when children show exploration of texture, movement or capabilities of sand.

**Sorting equipment**: when children make decisions, choosing appropriate equipment for the play they are undertaking.

**Modifying**: when children change their investigation to a more logical or successful one.

**Knowledgeable**: when play in the sand is informed, using knowledge previously gained from the play situation.

**Understanding**: the play shows knowledge as above but also indicates a further development of understanding.

**Communicative**: children discuss what they are doing in the sand with a leader developing the direction of the play.

**Recording**: children show early signs of recording their activities.

---

Fig. 7.6. Science potential in sand play
(Birchall, 1994)

## Activity 9 – Identifying learning through play

(Time required: 30 minutes)

Consider to what extent you have observed play of a similar nature to that outlined in Figure 7.6 when children are involved in play (structured or unstructured). Watch children as they play (perhaps with cars or with water) and note the scientific learning. You may like to use a proforma similar to the one below.

| Play Situation | Science Learning | Evidence (Children's comments or actions) |
|---|---|---|
|  |  |  |

Fig. 7.7.

**Activity 10 – Identifying science learning in other play situations**
(Time required: 30 minutes)
Using a different play situation, identify the potential scientific learning that could be encouraged through the materials provided or adult interaction. You may wish to consider an area within your classroom or select from the following: the art area; the outside play area; the garden; the construction area; or the role play area such as a shop, a garage, a garden centre, a clinic, a space station, a hairdressers, a post office or a travel agency.

## HOW DO WE ENCOURAGE COLLABORATIVE WORK WITH YOUNG CHILDREN?

Many teachers find that science is a useful area in which to develop children's collaborative skills. The exchange of ideas and the bringing together of minds to solve problems can help children to:

- understand concepts more clearly;

- develop communication skills;

- be tolerant with other children;

- see science as an area for fruitful collaboration.

The first activity on this subject is about examining the strategies used when people collaborate. This will have to be carried out with other people. The other two activities which focus on this area can, however, be carried out alone.

**Activity 11 – What is collaboration?**
(Time required: 45 minutes)
Resources:  —string;
            —plasticine to act as the bob;
            —dowel or a brush handle which can be used to support;
            —the pendulum.

One group of teachers should carry out the task outlined below. Two other people should act as observers and make notes about the actions and talk which they notice.

*Task*

- Make a pendulum.

- Play with it and talk about what you notice.

- Work together to find out whether the length of the string or the weight of the bob makes any difference to the swing.

Now, together with the observers, discuss the interaction in the group.

- Were tasks assigned?

- Who assumed the leadership role?

- Did everyone contribute to the talk?

- Did people listen to one another?

- Did everyone share ideas?

- Were people sensitive to others?

- Were a number of ideas considered before a decision was made?

- Did everyone agree with the decisions which were made?

- Would children have to use the same strategies and adopt similar roles?

## Activity 12 – Identifying strategies for developing collaboration

(Time required: 30 minutes)
List strategies that you would use to develop effective collaboration. For example:

- start with structured practical tasks;

- give the child who is talking a wooden spoon to hold;

- encourage children to look at the person who is talking;

- show children that you value their ideas;

- teach children how to deal with conflict.

What other strategies could you identify?

### Activity 13 – Planning to encourage collaboration
(Time required: 30 minutes)
Identify experiences that you could use to develop collaborative skills in a science context. For example:

- using sorting circles to classify rough and smooth objects;

- building a bridge between two chairs;

- using the computer and a program such as *Branch* or *Sorting Game* to sort a collection of leaves (see Chapter 10 for other suggestions for ICT).

### Activity 14 – Analysing collaboration
(Time required: 1 hour)
Watch groups of children as they carry out collaborative tasks and apply the criteria from Activity 11 in order to analyse the children's ability to work together effectively.

## WHAT ARE THE IMPORTANT STAGES IN PLANNING SCIENCE FOR YOUNG CHILDREN?

We have previously described the hypothetical case of Mrs Smith. We outlined her planning stages as she prepared for science with her combined Year 1 and Reception class (Bk. 1, Hartley and Macro, 7).

She takes into account the needs of the children and the school's long-term planning when preparing her plans for each half term. She also identifies assessment opportunities at this stage. Weekly and daily plans are then produced.

Many teachers plan in this way. However, we have discovered that many experienced teachers are concerned because they often find it impossible for every child to complete all the planned experiences. This can be a particular issue in the early years where maturity and concentration can vary considerably amongst the children. Teachers can tackle this by identification of the key ideas and skills which they want to develop. A series of related experiences might develop some of the same skills and concepts in a variety of contexts. By doing this they will be less likely to worry about every child completing all the tasks. This strategy also enables them to plan for differentiation and allows for a variety of learning styles.

## Activity 15 – Identifying contexts
(Time required: 30 minutes)
The key ideas that Mrs Smith planned to develop were:

*Reception* – that light comes from a source;
          – some materials allow light to pass through.

*Year 1* – shadows are formed when light does not pass through
        materials;
      – the light reflected from a flat, shiny surface (e.g. a mirror)
      produces an image.

The skills that Mrs Smith wished to develop were that children should
begin to:

*Reception* – make relevant observations;
          – suggest explanations about their observations.

| | Reception *Learning intentions* | *Structured play situation* | *Group with other adult* | *Mrs Smith's group* | *Whole class* |
|---|---|---|---|---|---|
| Wk one | Key idea: some objects allow light to pass through <br><br> Skill: make relevant observations | Exploring a variety of torches and objects in a darkened area of the room | Children sorting objects according to property of material: transparent, opaque, translucent | Selecting and testing fabrics for curtains in a model house | Introduce the topic through use of big book material and with reference to children's own experiences |
| Wk two | | | | | |
| | Year 1 <br> *Learning intentions* | *Play situation* | *Group with other adult* | *Mrs Smith's group* | *Whole class teaching* |
| Wk one | | | | | |
| Wk two | | | | | |

Fig. 7.8. An extract from Mrs Smith's initial plan

*Year 1* – understand when a test is fair;
     – make appropriate measurements;
     – interpret simple charts and tables prepared with the teacher.

Using the proforma in Figure 7.8, plan appropriate experiences to develop the key ideas and skills identified by Mrs Smith in her intentions for learning for a two-week period. You may assume that Mrs Smith spends one-and-a-half hours each week on science with either the whole class or with identified groups. The unsupervised play experiences and group work with another adult are in addition to this.

You may find the example of Figure 7.8 useful where Mrs Smith has identified the learning intentions for the first week and the children have an opportunity to develop their scientific learning in a variety of contexts.

## Activity 16 – Identifying contexts to develop key ideas
(Time required: 1 hour)
Consider your own children and plan work that will develop key ideas and skills in a variety of ways. Use the proforma as in Figure 7.9 if you wish.

| | **Reception** *Learning intentions* | *Structured play situation* | *Group with other adult* | *Teacher's group* | *Whole class* |
|---|---|---|---|---|---|
| Wk one | | | | | |
| Wk two | | | | | |
| | **Year 1** *Learning intentions* | *Play situation* | *Group with other adult* | *Teacher's group* | *Whole class teaching* |
| Wk one | | | | | |
| Wk two | | | | | |

Fig. 7.9. Planning proforma

## CONCLUSION

In this chapter we have discussed ways in which teachers might examine their own scientific thinking, plan an appropriate curriculum for early years science, identify learning through play and encourage children to develop scientific skills and concepts. We consider that science starts as soon as young children begin to explore their environment. Science has an important part to play in the holistic view of a child's early years education as well being a worthwhile subject in its own right.

## BIBLIOGRAPHY

Alexander, R., Rose, J. and Woodhead, C. (1992) *Curriculum Organisation and Classroom Practice in Primary Schools*, London: DES.

Birchall, L. (1994) How the Science Learning of Early Years Children could be Enhanced through Sand Play. Unpublished dissertation. Edge Hill University College.

Elstgeest, J. (1985) The right question at the right time, in W. Harlen (ed) *Primary Science: Taking the Plunge*, London: Heinemann.

Feasey, R. (1994) The challenge of science, in C. Aubrey (ed) *The Role of Subject Teaching in the Early Years of Schooling*, London: Falmer Press.

Graham, B. (1986) *Wheels: Science Early Learner Books*, Glasgow: Blackie.

Harlen, W., Holroyd, C. and Byrne, M. (1995) What effects do low confidence and low understanding have on teaching? in *Confidence and Understanding, Teaching Science and Technology*, Edinburgh Scottish Council for Research in Education, pp. 202–4.

NCC (1992) *Knowledge and Understanding of Science: Forces – A Guide for Teachers*. London: NCC.*

Shulman, L. S. (1987) Knowledge and teaching, *Harvard Educational Review*, Vol. 57, no. 1.

*Note*: This and other *Guides for Teachers* are available from SCAA. Contact: Customer Services Department, Newcombe House, 45 Notting Hill Gate, London W11 3JB. Other NCC titles include *Chemical Changes; Electricity and Magnetism; Energy; Genetics* and *Ecology*.

# 8
# Process Skills in Primary Science

*David Byrne*

## INTRODUCTION

This chapter builds upon the companion chapter in Book 1 (Bk. 1, Byrne, 8) by giving direct advice and assistance about approaches that will promote children's achievement in Science 1. The process skills within Science 1 are seen as presenting an opportunity to enhance science in primary education, to complement and further learning of science knowledge and understanding. The chapter assumes that your school has a science policy that promotes the need for and emphasis on process skills throughout the school. Schools vary considerably and so the chapter recognises the need for schools to tailor suggestions to suit their situation. The need for careful planning in science is stressed throughout. Examples of good practice given are drawn from ideas given trials in schools in the north west of England and north east Wales.

### Being wrong!

> Science is always wrong. It never solves a problem without creating ten more!
>
> (George Bernard Shaw)

The apprehension experienced by some teachers about problems associated with practical investigation in primary classrooms can seriously restrict the implementation of the Programmes of Study for Science 1. The fear of being wrong in science is one that we have all experienced. Science 1, however, should free us from such fears as there is rarely a single stock answer. Science 1 presents a marvellous opportunity for all children to achieve, and for abilities to be recognised. There is a considerable creative element to Science 1 seen when children of all ages begin to design investigations. Children usually approach science investigations and experiments positively and can work collaboratively to find a range of solutions. Therefore, teachers ought to approach Science 1 with a positive frame of mind.

From early infancy children carry out practical tasks, make decisions and enquire. Science education seeks progressively to focus and direct this activity so that decisions become increasingly informed and directed towards the children tackling their questions about the world. Progress across the school needs to be planned so that children develop these scientific abilities. Assessment of children's achievement in Science 1 can play an important part here, providing essential information to teachers who are then in a position to further the child's development in Science 1.

Science 1 is of particular value as it often motivates children who are somewhat disaffected and can make science work more meaningful for all. Science 1 can improve children's self-esteem, through achievement in a respected subject within which they can see that they have a role. The insight afforded to children by Science 1 is recognised to assist young children as they accommodate new scientific concepts (Harlen, 1992; Driver, 1983).

The teaching of Science 1 is required by legislation with 40 per cent of pupils' time in science being devoted to it (20 per cent to each of the other three 'content' or knowledge-based attainment targets). Findings in 1993/4 by the Office for Standards in Education (OFSTED) stated that planning in science was frequently weak with insufficient attention being given to whole-school planning and detail in Science 1. Where schools have dealt with the issue of whole-school planning for science, and particularly Science 1, then standards are often higher. The message from all quarters is that a thorough, systematic approach to planning and teaching science is required if there is to be continuity and progression in Science 1. Everyone needs to be involved including teachers and pupils. Teachers will have much to contribute, they require some ownership of changes and without doubt the policy or plan has to account for their personal needs. Children can be involved – we can talk to them about Science 1, and children can even use National Curriculum (NC) terminology. Children in Key Stage 1 have learned to use terms like 'Programme of Study' and 'learning objective'. Why not state to them clearly the purpose of a lesson in NC terms? This chapter advocates a clear whole-school approach, supported in classrooms by a systematic model

---

**SCIENCE MEDIUM-TERM PLANNING SHEET FOR KS1**

CLASS ........... TERM ........... TOPIC .............. AT/PoS .........

| **KNOWLEDGE PoS:** | **ACTIVITIES:** |
| --- | --- |
| *List PoS from Science 2/3/4 as required* | *Brief lists of activities to match PoS written in everyday language.* |

| **SKILLS:** | **ASSESSMENT:** |
| --- | --- |
| *List key skills to be targeted, maybe 3 maximum* | *Which targets are to be assessed?* |

**EVALUATION:**
*Comments for future reference offering constructive criticism.*

---

Fig. 8.1. Medium-term planning sheet KS1

---

**SCIENCE MEDIUM-TERM PLANNING SHEET FOR KS2**

CLASS ........... TERM ........... TOPIC ..............

| PoS FOR KNOWLEDGE: | KEY WORDS: |
|---|---|
| | *List words that need to be taught in topic.* |

**KEY ACTIVITIES:**
*Brief lists of activities for topic.*

**SCIENCE PROCESSES**

**FOCUS SKILLS**

1. **Planning experimental work**
   (a) to turn ideas suggested to them, and their own ideas into a form which can be investigated
   (b) that making predictions can be useful when planning what to do
   (c) to decide what evidence is to be collected
   (d) that changing one factor and observing or measuring the effect, whilst keeping other factors the same, allows a fair test or comparison to be made

*Use a highlighter pen to pick out skills especially linked to the activities planned. Not too many at a time! The way in which the highlighted skills are actually taught in the topic should be stated here.*

2. **Obtaining evidence**
   (a) to use simple apparatus and equipment correctly
   (b) to check observations and measurements by repeating them

3. **Considering evidence**
   (a) to use tables, bar charts and line graphs to present results
   (b) to make comparisons and to identify trends or patterns in results
   (c) to use results to draw conclusions
   (d) to indicate whether the evidence collected supports any prediction made
   (e) to try to explain conclusions in terms of scientific knowledge and understanding

**ASSESSMENT OPPORTUNITIES:**
*List target assessments to be made in both skills and knowledge. These are the learning outcomes:*

**COMMENTS:**

---

Fig. 8.2. Medium-term planning sheet KS2

which ensures that pupils are clear about what is expected of them in terms of science process and how they can achieve this.

## WHOLE-SCHOOL APPROACHES TO SCIENCE 1 PLANNING

The National Curriculum offers a skeleton for building a curriculum which will be a basic learning 'environment' through and in which children progress. Long-term planning across the primary years should identify learning outcomes not only for knowledge, but also for skills. Medium-term plans for each topic (frequently half-termly) need to include detail which will feed into short-term, weekly plans. The structure of the planning sheet can be vital here. The two examples of medium-term planning below offer differing models but both ensure that consideration to Science 1 is made (Figures 8.1 and 8.2).

### Activity 1 – Looking at planning

(Time required: 1–2 hours of lesson preparation)

Examine your medium-term plans for science (those that tell you and other teachers what topics or themes to cover in science and perhaps which elements of the Programme of Study you should teach). These will have been written by a team of staff including the co-ordinator for science. Ask yourself the following questions:

● How much detail is given about Science 1?

● Examine the Programme of Study for your age range. Are the school's medium-term plans addressing them?

● How will you turn these medium-term plans into short- term lesson or activity plans? The following checklist is offered as guidance:

| Checklist | Example |
| --- | --- |
| 1. Determine the Science 1 areas to be covered. | Fair testing |
| 2. Determine the content areas of science to be dealt with. | Friction |
| 3. Focus on a context which will be meaningful to the children. | Playground slides – sliding masses down a model slide (card covered in a shiny paper) |

101

| | |
|---|---|
| 4. Consider the time available and length of sessions. | 4 x 40 minutes |
| 5. Consider how the class will be organised | Whole class? Or some form of integration? |
| 6. Write your learning outcomes for Science 1. | That the children will: **identify** – control variables (slope, slide, surface, push, length of slope, etc); the thing they will change (the input variable), e.g. the material touching the slide; and the thing that will change as a result of the input variable, e.g. the distance the weight will travel at the bottom! |

You will need learning outcomes relating to friction.

Sketch out four lessons, for example:

*Lesson 1* – Introductory activity on friction, assess their understanding of fair testing, establish a question to promote investigations (where you identify misconceptions about friction, you may wish to introduce experiences in lesson 2 to challenge those misconceptions (see Chapter 2 in Books 1 and 2)).

*Lesson 2* – Children plan an investigation, you can differentiate by words of support and intervention.

*Lesson 3* – Carry out the investigation and examine results.

*Lesson 4* – Evaluate fairness of the test, record what you have done and evaluate methods. Identify weaknesses as future room for improvement.

Now plan the lessons in more detail. Be clear about what you intend for each session and how it will contribute to the whole. Make sure that children get the opportunity to discuss the scientific question to be answered. Can they (with guidance if required) form an hypothesis e.g. people wearing clothes made from smooth materials will travel further along the slide? Will they consider variables and how to control them? Their opportunity to predict what will happen is very important. Can the children suggest measures for the variables, e.g. for the mass should we measure in grams or kilos? How will they record the data? You may find Figure 8.3. of some value here particularly if you plan for different achievement groups in the class.

## STRANDS WITHIN SCIENCE 1

The long- and medium-term plans should address a number of themes within Science 1 which, if introduced and taught progressively, can lead to high achievement by a significant proportion of children. Some suggestions include:

- observation;
- question formation;
- prediction/hypothesis formation;
- fair testing;
- using equipment and resources – measuring, safety;
- compiling and presenting results;
- interpreting and concluding;
- evaluating investigations.

See Figure 8.3 for a little more detail, although please treat it with care as it is impossible to say how children will progress. It might be better for you to see Figure 8.3 as a starting point on which you will, as a school, improve. More advice on similar headings and progression within them can be found in Goldsworthy and Feasey (1994) and Allport *et al* (1993).

### Activity 2 – Science 1 strands
(Time required: 40 minutes)
Select a strand from Figure 8.3 that you feel comfortable with and look at either a lesson in science that you have recently taught or your plans for one you expect to teach. How was the strand developed? Did children show a range of capability in the strand? Did this strand affect another strand? For example, equipment available may influence the extent to which the test is fair.

Now select a strand about which you feel less secure and repeat this procedure.

| | Observation | Question formation | Prediction/ hypothesis | Fair testing |
|---|---|---|---|---|
| **Early primary** | simple observations | ask simple questions | simple predictions | can talk about fairness and lack of fairness |
| | similarity and difference | focus on the science in a context | prediction with some attempt to explain | can pick out elements which make a test fair |
| | describing | restate the teacher's questions | prediction with a reasonable explanation based on the child's experience | child becomes aware that several elements of a test need to be considered |
| | noticing features | | | |
| **Middle primary** | looking for relationships | based on the teacher's directions the child focuses questions on key variables | predictions begin to relates cause and effect | child will attempt to alter 1 variable |
| | identifying simple patterns focus on details | | explanations begin to use scientific ideas | the child can plan to control a number of variables just altering one |
| | | questions begin to be formulated as hypothesis | | |
| **Later primary** | select observation techniques | teacher identifies context for questions | prediction now has clear explanation which is expressed using scientific ideas | the child recognises variables to be controlled |
| | | child generates questions which can be approached in an investigation | | the child can plan reasonable values for these variables |

**Science 1**

Fig. 8.3. Possible progression in strands within Science 1

## Strands

| Equipment and resources | Results | Interpreting and concluding | Evaluating investigations |
|---|---|---|---|
| the child uses simple equipment | the child can describe what went on | the child can describe what went on | the child can say how well things went |
| the child compares and uses non-standard measures | the child experiences different ways of presenting results | the child can see simple cause and effect | the child can say whether they feel the test was a success |
| the child learns simple, safe procedures | the child gives some detail in oral accounts of tests | the child can say what happened and relate this to the prediction | the child can say whether the test was fair |
| the child begins to use simple standard measures | the child writes with increasing accuracy about tests | the child can show that one part of the test affected another | the child can identify a problem |
| the child uses a range of equipment and resources | different forms of presentation of results are discussed | the child can see that results support/refute conclusions | the child can suggest ways to improve the test |
| the child begins to exercise some choice | the child begins to make choices about how results should be presented | the child can describe patterns in the results | the child can say whether variables were controlled |
| the child lists equipment prior to use | | the child refers to science knowledge in the results | the child can say whether measures were accurate enough |
| the child uses equipment more accurately | the child includes results collection and presentation in plans for tests | the child can identify patterns in the results | |
| the child includes equipment in plans | the child calculates averages from results collected | the child uses patterns in the results to inform conclusions | the child can see that alternative conclusions can be drawn |
| the child sees the need to repeat measurements | the child uses results from tests to determine whether or not the test was useful | | the child can show how the test could be improved |
| the child selects appropriate equipment | | | |

In this or a future lesson try to develop, one, two or three of these strands.

## APPROACHES IN THE CLASSROOM

Good school planning helps teachers know where they are taking the children and by which route; children like to know where they are going. In terms of Science 1 a systematic approach within the classroom is important. For children to become scientific they need a structure to guide and support their work. Science 1 requires that pupils learn to act independently and that they should act with purpose. From an early age it will be useful for children to practise the language of Science 1.

Opportunities for children to develop these skills need to be built into the curriculum at regular intervals. Very often you will find that established science-based activities that are currently strongly teacher-directed can become more open-ended without dramatic change in methodology. This can be illustrated by the following example:

- children experimenting with fabrics to find out which are waterproof, the teacher with directing the pupils in their actions.

Whilst valuable in teaching basic skills this may not encourage independence. An alternate approach would be for the teacher to teach the basic skills and then to ask the children to predict which fabric they think will be the best (it is always important to clarify what you mean by 'best' – here it would need to be made clear: 'most waterproof'). The teacher would then provide resources enabling the children to devise a simple investigation to test out their prediction. Pupils may begin to apply their basic skills in that fair test in order to find an answer. Talking (Driver, 1983) in the form of discussion and guidance will contribute significantly to repeated and progressive experience in Science 1 as children move through school.

## SCIENCE 1 SUPPORT SHEETS

For children to become scientific, structure is needed to guide and support their work. Children can be supported in their Science 1 work by provision of simple support sheets. Schools that have introduced these at Key Stage 1 have seen most children achieving a promising degree of independence by the age of seven or eight. These sheets can come in many formats. What they do is provide a framework or system for pupils to work in. They can be:

● very content specific perhaps containing specific language relating to the investigation;

● somewhat structured;

● open-ended.

Such sheets encourage children towards an agreed view of the scientific process. It is hoped that the children's confidence will increase and teacher dependence will decrease.

Three stages are suggested in the construction of such support material:

1. supporting the planning stage
2. carrying out the test
3. after the test.

Copies of the three sections will combine to make a worthwhile tool for the child to see a test through. They will also provide some record of the child's achievement in Science 1. There will be times when teachers use only sheets from one stage and times when such sheets might all be used in one classroom to differentiate. The sheets are better used separately rather than given to a child all at the start. Examples for each stage are given in Figure 8.4. Different formats are provided for Key Stage 1, Key Stage 1/2 and Key Stage 2.

## Activity 3 – Science support sheets
(Time required: 1–2 hours)
Here we simply suggest that you try at least one of the support sheets provided in Figure 8.4. You might do this with a class or a group of children. We would suggest that you review its success with your learning objectives for Science 1 very much in mind. You might also look at the Programme of Study for Science 1 (DfE, 1995).

## SUPPORTING SCIENCE 1 THROUGH INTERVENTION

Careful planning is followed by the science in the classroom. The teacher's role is very important as it is more than enabling and providing a context. Teaching will involve the teacher in instructing, describing, clarifying, explaining, recalling, demonstrating,

| Science Process – Planning          Key Stage 1 | Science Process – Planning          Key Stage 1/2 | Science Process – Planning          Key Stage 2 |
|---|---|---|
| My Science About.................. | My Science Investigation about.................. | My Science Investigation of.................. |
| My science question is… | The question I want to answer is… | My question is…  My hypothesis is… |
| I think that this will happen: | I predict that: | I predict that… |
| The things that I will use: | My plan for the fair test. | My plan for a fair test. |
| What I will do: | The test will be fair because… | This is how I shall collect my results. |

Fig. 8.4. Proformas for children planning, testing and evaluating in Science 1

Science Process – The Test    Key Stage 1

My Science About. . . . . . . . . . . . . . . . . . . . . . . . . .

This is what I did.

We made it fair like this. . .

I found out that. . .

Science Process – The Test    Key Stage 1/2

My Science Investigation About. . . . . . . . . . . . . . . . . . .

This is what happened.

I did these things to make sure that it was fair.

My results were. . .

So now I know that. . .

Science Process – The Test    Key Stage 2

My Science Investigation of . . . . . . . . . . . . . . . . . . . .

This is what happened.

I controlled the variables to make it fair.
Input variables

Output variables

Control variable

My results were. . .

My results show that my prediction was. . .

So my hypothesis was. . .

These results tell me that. . .

109

| Science Process – After the Test  Key Stage 1 | Science Process – After the Test  Key Stage 1/2 | Science Process – After the Test  Key Stage 2 |
|---|---|---|
| My Science About............... is Finished | My Science Investigation ............... is Over | My Science Experiment About........ is Complete |
| Was I right or wrong? | My prediction was…  This is because | Was my prediction correct?  Was my hypothesis correct? |
| My result was… | My results told me… | What did I find out? |
| I can now find out more now by… | I have found out that… | Could I improve on this test? |
|  | If I did this again I would… | How could I find out more? |

questioning, prompting, interpreting, illustrating, evaluating, predicting, eliciting, speculating, previewing, reviewing (Richards, 1996). The most effective teachers do all these things without robbing the child of a sense of ownership of and role within the science. Almost all of these behaviours above are forms of communication and as such are two-way. It is worth taking a little time to look at how you use these in teaching Science 1. Questioning is a good place to start as there has been previous writing in this area (Harlen, 1992; Elstgeest, 1985).

## Activity 4 – Teachers' questions
(Time required: 2 hours)
Here we will focus on your questions to the children. We are going to suggest that you look at your questions to determine whether they are open or closed, and what contribution the two kinds make in Science 1.

### Part A: Planning
Here we suggest that you make your questions a significant part of your planning. In a lesson you should identify at least one point when you will intervene to further your lesson objectives. After reviewing the lesson objectives, write a number of questions which you might put to the children, such as:

- Who can tell us what we've been doing in science?

- How will we find out why the animals like the dark?

- Which ball bounced most often?

- Will this test be fair?

Make a note of which ones are open and which are closed questions. Now evaluate your questions.

### Part B: Evaluating questions
For this part you will need to audio-tape record that part of a lesson that includes the questions from you (10–20 minutes will be enough). Play back the tape without stopping it. Do you get an overall view of who is leading? Who is contributing? Now go back to particular points where questions elicited responses. How did the questions do? Did children respond differently? Were open and closed questions

performing different functions? Was one form better than another for Science 1?

If you wish to find out more about the power of questions in science you might like to read Shiela Jelly or Jos Elstgeest in Harlen (1985) or Wynne Harlen herself (1992).

All forms of teacher intervention are significant. A sound basis can be found in the approach to science spelt out in Book 1 by Schilling and McGuigan.

## ASSESSING SCIENCE 1

Assessment of Science 1 needs to start early in the year so that coupled with evidence of earlier work you can make your expectations challenging but realistic. Assessment in Science 1 will need to be repeated during the year with perhaps a change in focus so that through the year you touch on each part of Science 1 at least once with each child. Such expectations should be stated in either your school science policy or policy for assessment, recording and reporting.

The route to good assessment is planning. If the learning objectives are clearly spelt out during the planning stage then it is easier to establish whether or not the targets have been achieved. Science 1 is a challenging area to assess because it is active and often hard to catch on paper. Achievement can also be context related so that children who have achieved well might appear to 'slip back'.

Don't forget that the children can assess themselves. They are usually honest and accurate if you take the time to share the objectives with them. See Ron Ritchie's thoughts on this and other assessment matters in Chapter 9.

A simple record will allow you to track coverage of Science 1 by groups and the whole class. You ought to focus at least some of your valuable time on making detailed comments on the children who surprise you, i.e. their achievement outside (either above or below) the range you expected.

## HOW IS EVIDENCE COLLECTED

Much of the assessment at both Key Stages is based upon the knowledge of the child gained during everyday interactions in the classroom. Careful planning should ensure that the skills to be assessed are clearly targeted. These targets give a clear focus about what is to be assessed. In a busy lesson the specific skill to be assessed is known so it is possible to direct tasks or observations more effectively. You are very much a detective gathering clues in a variety of ways. These may include one or a combination of the following:

- listening to the words that children say to both you and each other;

- gauging the way children tackle problems and carry out investigations;

- observing behaviour displayed by children, e.g. perseverance, level of concentration, co-operation, etc.;

- marking written, graphical or diagrammatic work for the quality and content;

- observing the level of independence in individuals;

- looking at the drawings of plans to indicate a child's ability to see accurately and represent their observations; sequences of drawings to explain events are particularly useful;

- using the planning sheets to find those who can predict, plan, record and evaluate;

- reading evaluations and conclusions in order to establish the level of insight displayed.

### Activity 5 – Collecting evidence about Science 1
(Time required: 1 hour)
With your learning outcomes for Science 1 clearly in mind, look at samples of work from four children to determine whether you can find evidence as to how the children have achieved. This activity will be added to considerably if you can find time to talk to the children about their work. Make sure you have your learning objectives clearly in mind.

## GATHERING EVIDENCE

It is not necessary to have detailed evidence for every child; some evidence for each child is, however, desirable. Samples very often appear to have little value at first but as time goes on, and a child moves through school, samples of work do show progress and can indicate peaks and troughs in achievement and can be used in discussion with parents and other interested adults, e.g. SEN teachers or if colleagues' assessment is challenged! It is not possible to have collected evidence for some areas of Science 1 especially at Key Stage

1. So it is sensible to gather what is more easily collected and manageable. Try to gather one piece of work for each child in Science 1 on a termly basis. Store it in either an individual folder or profile or in a class folder. A sample of work including Science 1 is collected on a termly basis and one sample from the other attainment targets in the term in which they arise.

### Activity 6 – Keeping a record
(Time required: 1 hour)
Now will be a good time to review your present system of recording achievement in Science 1.

● Do you have a system for recording coverage of Science 1?

● Does it match with other science records?

● How does the system cope with children who fall outside your expectations?

It is not possible to keep cumulative records of each child's work as they move through the school as it would become cumbersome and inefficient. One solution is to drop one term's evidence each term, e.g. as evidence from this year's term 3 is collected, last year's term 3 sample is removed so in effect you always have three terms' work available! Some schools operate a six-term version of this model. The time-consuming part of any system is the dating of the work coupled with a brief comment about the context, but this is vital if the collection is going to have any value. It may be possible to target a piece of work well in advance, which is chosen to be the sample once a term so that you are prepared and mark it with clear dates and comments.

A school portfolio of Science 1 can be valuable but only if it is used as a means of supporting and/or helping you and your colleagues make judgments about the levels that are being given to the children. Samples of work demonstrating a level can support in-house discussions and moderation.

## CONCLUSION

Science 1 is for many the most important part of the science curriculum in primary schools. It gives children the chance to work in a scientific way and skills and processes give meaning to the knowledge being learnt. Science 1 motivates children allowing them to use their imagination and heightening the opportunities for knowledge and understanding to deepen. And yet Science 1 remains one of the more difficult areas to teach. Science 1 is still under pressure in the National Curriculum from perceived lack of time and from the current national assessment model which is knowledge-based. This chapter coupled with Chapter 8 in Book 1 aims to remove some of the mystery that many still feel about the practical aspects of primary science. It sets out the argument that Science 1 remains vital for each child's curriculum and gives both background information and ideas for systems that may be put into place in a primary school in order to make it work. It is easy to become impatient; it takes time for children to be able to work independently and sensibly with purpose and a sense of achievement. Systems such as planning for progression in Science 1, giving pupils support sheets, methods of assessment and ways of gathering samples will assist but will take time to establish.

## BIBLIOGRAPHY

Allport, G. (*et al*) (1993) *The Sc1 Book: Investigations 5–16*, Northampton: Northamptonshire Inspection and Advisory Service.

Department for Education (1995) *Science in the National Curriculum*, London: HMSO.

Driver, R. (1983) *The Pupil as Scientist*, Milton Keynes: Open University Press.

Elstgeest, J. (1985) The right question at the right time, in W. Harlen *Primary Science: Taking the Plunge*, London: Heinemann.

Goldsworthy, A. and Feasey, R. (1994) *Making Sense of Primary Science Investigations*, Hatfield: Association of Science Education.

Harlen, W. (1985) *Primary Science: Taking the Plunge*, London: Heinemann.

Harlen, W. (1992) *The Teaching of Science*, London: David Fulton.

Richards, C. (1996) *Address to the 10th Annual North West Primary Advisers' Conference*, Manchester, Education Management–North West.

# 9
# Implementing Assessment and Recording as a Constructive Process

*Ron Ritchie*

## INTRODUCTION

This chapter offers guidance and strategies to support teachers in treating assessment and recording of science as a constructive process. It begins with an analysis of the opportunities for assessing science skills (linked to Science 1 within the National Curriculum). These are linked to the different phases of the framework for teaching, based on a constructivist view of learning, introduced in Book 1 (Bk. 1, Ritchie, 9). This is provided to inform work related to the next activity and to offer a 'tool' for teachers to support their ongoing teacher assessments of children's learning in science. The chapter includes a number of staff development activities intended to:

- improve teachers 'assessment skills';

- explore ways of encouraging children to self-assess (particularly in the area of Sc. 1);

- introduce concept-mapping as a tool for assessing children;

- critically analyse and evaluate current approaches to record-keeping in science to improve that practice.

In each of these areas, background information and further references can be found in the companion book (Bk. 1, Ritchie, 9).

## OPPORTUNITIES FOR ASSESSING SKILLS AT DIFFERENT STAGES OF A CONSTRUCTIVIST APPROACH

Figure 9.1 is a table showing skills that might be assessed during orientation, elicitation/structuring, intervention/restructuring, review and application phases of a teaching approach based on a constructivist view of learning. The table uses statements from the Programmes of Study linked to Key Stages 1 and 2. These are, of course, not intended to be criteria for assessment and simply indicate aspects of scientific skills that should be taught. However, this provides a clear indication of the potential for assessment when these Programmes of Study are being experienced by the children (which is perhaps a more useful phrase than 'delivered by the teacher' when considering assessment). The numbers and letters relate to those used in the National Curriculum document (DfE, 1995, pages 2–3 and 7–8). The label Sc. 1 refers to the PoS related to Experimental and Investigative Science; Sc. 0 refers to the general requirements for each Key Stage which apply across all areas of science (Sc. 1–4) and cover systematic enquiry, science in everyday life, the nature of scientific ideas, communication and health and safety. These have been included because they include aspects of scientific skills.

## DEVELOPING TEACHERS' SKILLS IN ASSESSMENT

The importance of teachers developing appropriate assessment skills was stressed in Chapter 9 of Book 1. These skills involve focused observation, active listening, responsive questioning and the skill of recognising significance amongst the overwhelming amount of information that a teacher can potentially gather in a classroom concerning children's learning. The quality of the judgments that teachers make is the key to effective assessment. This section outlines a staff development activity intended to develop such skills. It is based on a strategy which has been used regularly by the author and his colleagues when working with teachers, headteachers and students. The activity encourages practitioners to focus on a small group of children and collect intensive data from which they identify evidence of significance and analyse the quality of their interactions with the group or individuals within it. It is intended to provide teachers with an opportunity to examine their own practice in detail. It does not, of course, mirror what can realistically happen on a daily basis in the busy classroom. However, experience suggests that an activity such as

117

| Phase of teaching/learning | Link to Programmes of Study (KS1) | Link to Programmes of Study (KS2) |
|---|---|---|
| **Orientation** Arousing children's interests and curiosity | Sc.0 1a – ask questions<br><br>Sc.0 1c – use both first-hand experience and simple secondary sources | Sc.0 1a – ask questions<br><br>Sc.0 1C – use both first-hand experience and secondary sources |
| **Elicitation/Structuring** Helping children to find out and clarify what they already know and think | Sc.1 2a – to explore using appropriate senses<br>Sc.1 2b – to make observations and measurements<br>Sc.1 3c – to make simple comparisons<br><br>Sc.0 1b – used focused exploration . . . to acquire scientific . . . skills | Sc.0 1b – used focused exploration . . . to acquire scientific . . . skills<br>Sc.1 1a – to turn ideas—into a form that can be investigated<br>Sc.1 1b – that making predictions can be useful when planning<br>Sc.1 1c – to decide what evidence should be collected |
| **Intervention/ Restructuring** Encouraging children to test out their ideas, to extend, develop or replace them | Sc.1 1a – to turn ideas . . . into a form that can be investigated<br>Sc.1 1b – that thinking about what is expected to happen can be useful when planning<br><br>Sc.1 1c – to recognise when a test or comparison is unfair<br><br>Sc.1 2c – to make a record of observations and measurements<br><br>Sc.0 1d – use IT to collect, store . . . information<br><br>Sc. 13b – to use drawings, tables and bar charts to present results<br><br>Sc.1 3d – to use results to draw conclusions | Sc.1 1d – that changing one factor . . . whilst keeping others the same, allows a fair test or comparison to be made.<br><br>Sc.1 1e – to consider what apparatus or equipment to use<br><br>Sc.1 2b – to make careful observations and measurements<br>Sc.1 2c – to check observations and measurements by repeating them<br><br>Sc.0 1d – use IT to collect, store . . . information<br><br>Sc.1 3a – to use tables, bar charts and line graphs to present results<br>Sc.1 3b – to make comparisons . . . identify trends or patterns<br>Sc.1 3c – to use results to draw conclusions |
| **Review** Helping children to recognise the significance of what they have found out | Sc.0 4a/b – use scientific vocabulary/present information in a number of ways | Sc.0 4a/b – use scientific vocabulary/present information in an appropriate and systematic manner |
| **Application** Helping children to relate what they have learnt to everyday life | Sc.1 3e – to indicate whether the evidence supports any predictions made<br><br>Sc.1 3f – to try to explain what they found out<br><br>Sc.0 2a – relate . . . science to domestic and environmental contexts | Sc.1 3d – to indicate whether the evidence supports predictions made<br>Sc.1 3e – to try to explain conclusions<br><br>Sc.0 2a – explain and interpret a range of familiar phenomena |

Fig. 9.1. Opportunities for assessment of Science 1

that outlined (especially if repeated) does help teachers become more effective assessors in the normal classroom situation – they become more aware of the significance of their role; more focused in their questioning; more sensitive to the variety and unexpected nature of children's ideas. Ideally it should be carried out collaboratively with a colleague and this may involve seeking support from the headteacher to provide an opportunity for two teachers to work together. It can be organised as a whole-staff activity on an in-service day (having one or two classes in school for the morning to provide the children). Crucial to the success of the activity is the need for decisions and (where it is possible) discussion to be based on evidence rather than impression. The task can be completed in one morning, or spread over a few days.

## Activity 1 – Developing skills for assessing science
(Time required: 1 hour)
(a) Plan an activity (with a colleague's help) for a small group of children (approximately 4–6). The activity should involve opportunities for you to elicit the children's current understanding and/or the scientific skills that they can use – it should be exploratory and open-ended. Work with a collection of items (e.g. vegetables, moving toys, fabrics) would be suitable. The activity should last 20–30 minutes. During the planning, clarify (and write down) the skills that you hope to encourage the children to use (observation, comparing, sorting, classifying, raising questions, predicting, discussing and reporting, recording and making notes, etc.) and the ideas that might be developed (e.g. the properties and uses of fabrics). You might also consider some of the questions you will ask.

(b) Implement the activity at a time when you can work with the small group uninterrupted (which may mean using assembly time, break or singing practice). You should teach the group whilst your colleague observes, collecting as much data as possible concerning what you and the children say and do. The children will need to be told about your colleague's role and she should avoid eye contact and talking to the group if possible – children soon accept this. The data collected should be unedited at this stage, but all contributions should be (as far as possible) named. A data collection sheet is included as Figure 9.2. If it is not possible to recruit a colleague or helper for this, an alternative is to audio-tape the session.

119

| | Page: | Time: |
|---|---|---|
| Initials | Utterances/Actions | Comments |
| 1 | | |
| 2 | | |
| 3 | | |
| 4 | | |
| 5 | | |
| 6 | | |
| 7 | | |
| 8 | | |
| 9 | | |
| 10 | | |
| 11 | | |
| 12 | | |
| 13 | | |
| 14 | | |
| 15 | | |
| 16 | | |
| 17 | | |
| 18 | | |
| 19 | | |
| 20 | | |
| 21 | | |
| 22 | | |
| 23 | | |
| 24 | | |
| 25 | | |
| 26 | | |
| 27 | | |
| 28 | | |
| 29 | | |
| 30 | | |
| 31 | | |
| 32 | | |
| 33 | | |
| 34 | | |
| 35 | | |
| 36 | | |
| 37 | | |
| 38 | | |
| 39 | | |
| 40 | | |
| 41 | | |
| 42 | | |
| 43 | | |
| 44 | | |
| 45 | | |
| 46 | | |
| 47 | | |
| 48 | | |
| 49 | | |
| 50 | | |

Fig. 9.2. Data collection sheet

(c) Before referring to the data, write down and discuss your immediate impressions of how the session went, how the children responded, your role and what you learnt about them. Be specific about the latter, if possible.

(d) Now go back over the data carefully and analyse what was actually said and done. Do not rush this, and think about the significance of each contribution and what motivated and informed it. What does this tell you about the children's skills, ideas and the nature of your interactions with them? Be specific about the evidence you have to show their learning. The table (Figure 9.1) may help at this stage. Write out a summary for one or two children making explicit reference to the evidence. For example, if you think the child is predicting, cite the actual words used. Compare this account with your first impressions – are there any differences and if so why?

(e) Discuss with the observer, after this analysis, ways in which you, as teacher (and assessor), could have been more effective. Plan a second activity, in the light of the evidence collected, to move the children forward in their learning. In this way you are seeking to use the evidence in a genuinely formative way. Identify ways in which the teacher's role can be improved.

(f) Implement the second activity (on the same day or at some later date) with the same group. You could swap roles for this second activity. Collect and analyse the data as before.

(g) Identify ways in which lessons learnt from this intensive activity could be applied to your normal teaching situation. Plan to implement any change in practice that you consider appropriate and monitor your own work over a period of time to allow you to reflect on your success.

*Note*
It is worth stressing again, that this activity is not offered as an example of how to do assessment in the classroom. No one could collect data like this in everyday teaching. It is intended to help teachers develop skills including: focused observation, sensitivity to meanings behind what children say and do, elicitation skills (helping children to become aware of and clarify their own ideas), selectivity (the ability to identify

actions and utterances which provide insights into learning) and responsiveness (the ability to use assessment information to inform future questions and plans).

## ENCOURAGING SELF-ASSESSMENT

Encouraging children to carry out self-assessments can provide a surprising source of evidence to support a teacher's assessment. Children, even very young ones, are capable of making judgments about their own learning. However, to do it well they need practice, they need to work in a supportive, non-threatening ethos and they need to have the language that will enable them to be specific about their learning. Too often in classroom situations, only the teacher has a clear idea of the learning outcomes intended for an activity. Children may completely misunderstand these if they are not made explicit – for example, concentrating on neatness of presentation when the teacher's goal relates to science skills. The following staff-development activity focuses on this aspect of assessment and is likely to require one or two hours work outside the normal classroom routine.

### Activity 2 – Encouraging children to self-assess in science
(Time required: 1–2 hours)

(a) Select an activity you intend the children to tackle that involves them carrying out an investigation (or other activity) during which they will use a range of skills.

(b) Clarify criteria that will indicate the success of the children in completing the investigation. With older or more experienced learners it may be appropriate to negotiate these criteria with the children. Decide how best to communicate these to the children before they tackle the activity.

(c) Share the criteria for success with the children before they start an activity in an appropriate way.

(d) When they have completed an investigation, ask them to review their work and self-assess using the criteria you set. Encourage them to comment on other achievements, and weaknesses, beyond

122

these criteria, if they can. You may find a sample proforma helpful with older children, or the use of symbols with younger ones. Figure 9.3 provides an example for you to modify to your own purpose (it is unlikely that you will wish the children to answer all of these example questions).

---

### Thinking about my science work

My name:                                          Date:

I worked with:

What was your investigation about?

What did you want to find out?

How did you decide what to do?

Did you make predictions before you planned your work – did they prove correct?

What factor did you decide to change?

What did you decide to measure or observe?

What did you decide to keep the same?

Do you think you chose the right ones?

In what ways did you try and make your test fair?

How did you make your measurements as careful as possible?

Were you careful in recording your results?

In what ways were you pleased with the way you recorded your results?

How did you present your results and findings – was it the best way?

What interesting things did you find out or learn?

---

What was good about the way your group worked?

What would you like to do next to find out more?

How could you improve your science work next time?

Fig. 9.3. Self-assessment proforma

(e) Use these self-assessments to evaluate the success of the activity and your skills in making the learning goals explicit to the children.

You can use the insights that you have gained through this activity to help you decide on other ways in which you could build more self-assessment into the children's classroom work.

## USING CONCEPT-MAPPING

Many teachers who explore the use of concept-mapping with their children find that it proves a useful means of gaining assessment evidence that is hard to obtain in other ways. Concept maps can be used:

- at the start of a programme of work to elicit existing ideas;
- during, to help the children clarify their developing ideas (and the teacher to monitor them);
- at the end to assess what children have learnt and to support them in reviewing their own learning.

The following activity is designed to encourage a teacher to try out concept-mapping. It is designed to link with on-going classroom work but will involve an additional one or two hours of a teacher's time outside the classroom.

## Activity 3 – Encouraging the use of concept-mapping
(Time required: 1–2 hours)

(a) Select a science topic that the children are about to study. With the whole class, or a smaller group, brainstorm words related to the topic that they already know. For example, a topic on 'floating and sinking' could lead to: heavy, balanced, shape, light, air, bubbles, gaps, materials.

(b) Ask the children to choose two words which are linked in some way (in the whole group, or in pairs) and ask them to think about the link and tell you (or write down) what that link is. Share these and discuss the variety of ideas and how they show what everybody thinks.

(c) Tell the children that you want them to draw a 'picture' or map of their own ideas on which they can only put words that link together in some way. They should try and write on a line between the words explaining how they think they link. One word can have several links. Stress that there are no right answers, that you are interested in all their ideas, and that the 'shape' of the map is for them to decide. You may find that a class map helps them understand what is required, although it will undoubtedly influence their own outcomes. You could produce a class map in a related but different area, or using different words. The children may find it less threatening if they work in pairs initially. Allow them to add their own words or leave out ones that they cannot link from the brainstormed list.

(d) As the children are working on these, circulate and probe the children, sensitively, about their maps (perhaps adding, for them, amplifications that they give orally). Encourage them to add new links, or even to start again if they have reached 'dead-ends' or the shape organisation of their maps is proving unhelpful as they seek to develop them.

(e) Analyse the maps for the insights they provide into the children's existing ideas. Do they indicate alternative ideas, do they show the children know more than you think? Are they all a similar shape? (Sophisticated maps are usually hierarchical rather than like spokes from a central word.) Is there a pattern to the number of links and the sophistication of the children's ideas? Figure 9.4 provides an example for you to consider alongside those of your children.

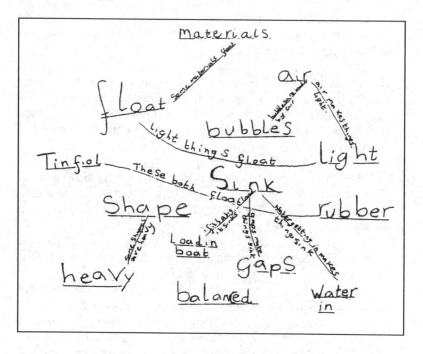

Fig. 9.4. Concept map on floating and sinking

In the light of this first attempt to get the children to produce concept maps, reflect on how it could be used in other ways within your teaching. Consider the ways in which children might be supported in producing more sophisticated maps as they progress through a school – what might progression in concept-mapping look like? Consider the benefits of getting the children to talk to each other about their maps. What strategies could be used to support learners with special educational needs, or those whose ideas are more advanced than their writing skills?

## EVALUATING EXISTING APPROACHES TO RECORD-KEEPING

Each school has its own approach to record-keeping in science. There is no 'right answer' to the best kind of record and for that reason this chapter does not include exemplar records. In some ways, the most useful record, for formative purposes, is a blank sheet of paper on which a teacher records in narrative form, with dates, significant evidence of a child's learning and includes an indication of the intended action resulting from the insights gained from the evidence. So many of the complex tick box records devised by schools in the past have done little more than record that a child has had an experience: they provide little evidence of what the child learnt from the experience. Of more importance is the need for teachers to reassure themselves that the records that they use are appropriate to their purpose, that the minimum statutory requirements are met, and that the approach is efficient and as useful as possible. The following activity focuses on an evaluation of existing practice in order to support action planning for new or revised approaches (if needed). It is best carried out as a whole-staff activity (or is even better if it involves staff from more than one school). It will involve a minimum of one two-hour meeting, ideally two, or part of an in-service day, with individuals spending time before collecting together examples.

### Activity 4 – Evaluating record-keeping used in science
(Time required: 2 hours+)

(a) Collect together examples of records maintained by colleagues in the area of science. Include informal records (in teacher notebooks), annotation sheets and annotated samples of work, class records, planning records, record sheets (for formative and summative use), pupils' own records (e.g. charts or tables of activities in the back of a book), children's self-assessment records, report forms, elements of profiles, etc.).

(b) Clarify the purpose for different kinds of records and establish criteria for evaluating them. Distinguish records which tell you what children have done (which may more efficiently be a class record) from what they have learnt (an individual record). Distinguish formative, summative, diagnostic and evaluative purposes of records. How regularly should records be updated?

Who should contribute to or see them? What evidence or reference to evidence should/do the records include? What records are needed when a child changes class/school? What records are needed to inform statutory requirements, annual reports and parent interviews? How will children's achievements against NC level descriptions be recorded? Should records for Sc. 1 be more detailed than records for Sc. 2–4?

(c) Evaluate the collected records against the appropriate criteria (perhaps with a colleague to feedback to the whole staff).

(d) From this analysis identify strengths and weaknesses of the current approach. Are there gaps in the system? Are there records which are redundant or duplicated? Do any records serve a genuine formative purpose? Is the system as practical and efficient as it could be? Could the pupils or their parents be more involved in record-keeping?

(e) Use the analysis above to decide on an action plan to refine or improve your record-keeping in science. Decide on a manageable step forward and plan to introduce the change and monitor its development.

## CONCLUSION

Teaching science involves several inextricably linked elements that include: preparing and implementing plans, interacting with children, assessing and recording. Any attempt to improve professional practice in the area of assessment and record-keeping will have implications in all the other areas. Effective assessment requires effective classroom management. To assess, teachers need to spend 'quality' time with individuals and groups. This is only possible in a well-organised and managed classroom.

This chapter has provided strategies to support teachers in improving their assessment practice, but they should be seen as starting points, or as part of a long-term process, not as solutions. They are not intended, in any way, to be prescriptive and should be adapted to meet your individual needs or those of your school. Improving practice in terms of assessment and record-keeping will best be implemented in the context of whole-school developments and an agreed assessment policy. For example, it is more difficult to develop self-assessment skills in children if such approaches are not valued and supported in other classes – the school ethos is significant. Progression in science by individual children will be greatly enabled by continuity of practice throughout the school. Consequently the activities and strategies introduced in this chapter will be most successful if explored in a collaborative way by all the staff in a school. In that way, it will be possible to come to a shared understanding of each others' values concerning assessment and recording and agree on a common approach which should, as its key goal, seek to improve the quality of children's learning in science.

## BIBLIOGRAPHY

Department for Education and the Welsh Office (1995) *Science in the National Curriculum*, London: HMSO.

# 10
# Information and Communication Technology (ICT) in Primary Science

*Alan Cross and Tony Birch*

## INTRODUCTION

> Pupils should be given opportunities, where appropriate, to develop and apply their information technology (IT) capability in their study of science.
>
> (DfE, 1995, p. 1)

This chapter aims to assist primary teachers and curriculum managers to use information and communication technology (ICT) in teaching science. The activities can be used in the classroom or by science curriculum managers to further the use of ICT in science throughout the school.

Commonly, in the world outside education, scientific activity takes place with the support of ICT. We believe that ICT:

- improves the accuracy, reliability and speed of investigations, and no doubt it affects the variety and even the quality of scientific investigation;

- is just as appropriate in the science pursued by young children in primary education;

- in science is best characterised as a tool for young children through which to promote investigation and learning.

# PROMOTING LEARNING IN SCIENCE THROUGH ICT

Scientific activities are very powerful, practical situations in which children explore questions that require investigation. ICT can contribute by making questions more approachable, by helping the child seek a solution and communicate with others about the scientific process and its results.

| ICT can contribute by: | Example |
|---|---|
| Storing and presenting texts and charts clearly and accurately. | Record and present data and observations from an investigation into the effects of wing spans on paper gliders. |
| Using and storing text which can be added to, for communication about progress and results. | Communicate the changes in growth of seedlings through the use of a word processor or text handler. |
| Simulating the real world to investigate ideas which are difficult to explore first-hand. | Investigate decisions made during the life of a badger through a computer-based model/simulation, e.g. *Badger Trails.* |
| Learning about environments not accessible in any other way. | Investigate the workings of the human body through an interactive computer-based encyclopaedia giving a visual representation, e.g. *The Ultimate Human Body.* |
| Measuring light, sound, temperature, PH. | Sensing the amount of light at various depths in a pond. |

How often are the suggestions in the box above used in your science lessons? We suggest that where possible readers should carry out a review of their own practice prior to asking colleagues to do the same. The focus in the activities moves from the classroom to the whole school with emphasis on progression in both ICT and science.

131

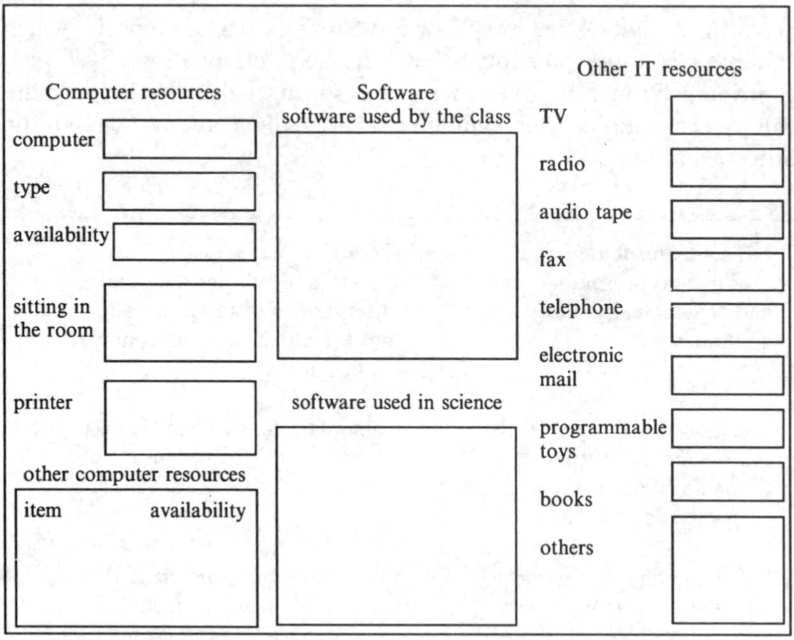

Fig. 10.1. Classroom ICT audit

## Activity 1 – Let's find out about this classroom

(Time required: 1–2 hours)

It is essential that you have a clear picture of what is going on now. Use Figures 10.1 and 10.2 to conduct an audit. The audit in Figure 10.1 will encourage you to look at the classroom. You should be able to determine a picture of the availability of resources. However, it is also very important that you look at the work of the children and talk to them about both their ICT and their science.

Figure 10.2 will assist with this as the focus of the activity is more on the science that the children are doing. By the end of this activity you may have developed a number of further questions to ask; for example:

● Is there an option to print graphs on a piece of software?

● How should we group children for ICT in science?

● Can this equipment be safely moved?

| Classroom audit | | |
|---|---|---|
| In my classroom do the children: | When do the children do this? | How often Examples this year? |
| Do science? | | |
| Use the computer? | | |
| Use the computer to:<br>  handle text?<br>  create pictures/diagrams?<br>  handle data?<br>  present data? | | |
| Use ICT to help draw a conclusion to the investigation? | | |

Fig. 10.2. An audit of computer use in the classroom

Keep a note of these. Some will be easy to answer. Others a little harder! Answers do exist! Who can assist you? Perhaps the ICT co-ordinator? The science co-ordinator? Another member of staff? Is there an LEA ICT consultant? Are there tutors at a local university? Perhaps there is a publication? What about the equipment or software supplier? Does software exist to support part of your science curriculum?

## Activity 2 – Let's do some science!
(Time required: 1–2 hours spread over one day or two)
It is important to see the potential of ICT in science before we move to other matters. It is likely that as a primary teacher you will be involved in teaching some science in the coming term. We hope that both you and the children are familiar with a word processor or texthandler (e.g. *Phases, Pages, Pendown, Impression*).

You will have seen examples of children writing on the computer just after they have completed the science. However, there is much more potential. We would like you to experiment with other phases of the investigation process and see how much ICT has to offer.

This activity is about more than simply writing about a science investigation. We are suggesting that ongoing stages, decisions and thoughts will be noted and developed on the computer.

---

*Note*

It is worth exploring the texthandler you intend to use to see if it has a note pad (see Figure 10.3). This is an optional window which can appear on the screen if you wish. It allows you to have a collection of relevant words and phrases on the screen. Both you and the children can add words and phrases to the note pad. These might include for Science 1: fair test, observe, we predicted that . . . and we measured the . . . , etc. and for a focus on energy might include: the ability to do work, conserved, energy transfer, stored, movement energy and friction.

---

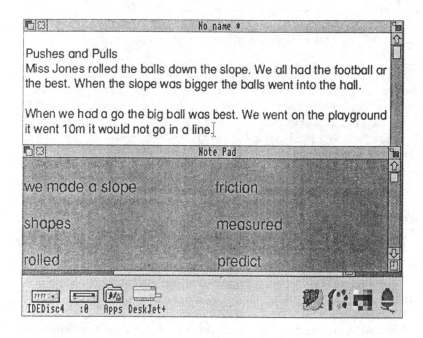

Fig. 10.3. Page from *Phases* texthandler showing note pad

| Science process | ICT contribution | Example |
|---|---|---|
| As teacher establish the context. | Teacher uses computer for planning and resource preparation. | Musical instruments – amplification |
| Discuss and brainstorm a series of questions. Encourage a wide range of questions. | In pairs children brainstorm 10 questions. These are noted in an ICT document. They then select one or two which could be investigated in the classroom. | 10 questions<br>– would larger elastic bands be louder?<br>– would a large shell help?<br>– try placing the instrument in a container<br>– move the instrument nearer?<br>– do larger ears help?<br>– does the person make a difference?<br>– are all larger instruments louder?<br>– does the material of the box matter?<br>– hit it/pluck it harder?<br>– metal instruments are louder? |
| Select a question and brainstorm for an investigation. | Highlight the question. Print out in large text. Add some clarification, a prediction. | Putting the instrument in a container<br>– different containers<br>– a fair test?<br>– different materials?<br>– measuring sound? |
| Plan the scientific investigation. | The children construct a flow chart on the computer. | First we will...<br>Then we will...<br>It will be fair because...<br>We will record data like this... |
| Conduct the investigation<br>– observe – record<br>– measure – test. | Record on computer in appropriate form. |        1st try  2nd try<br>big     60      55<br>medium  50      50 |
| Present the conclusions and perhaps an account of the investigation. | Here we might start a new file or edit the original. The original or working file will be an excellent record. | We found that... |

Fig. 10.4. An example of ICT within a science investigation

First you will need to establish what science you are doing. For this activity you will need to be addressing Science Process (Sc. 1). Have a look at Figure 10.4 and select part of or the whole science process. Then select a group of children (the size will depend on the computer access) to whom you can fairly confidently give access to the computer. It may be worth providing this group with their own directory on the hard disc. It will certainly assist you if they can load and save files themselves. If they cannot, consider training one or two children in the group to do so and then train them to train and assist the others. The objective then is to ask the children to write a document over a prolonged period, at least the timespan of the investigation. In some cases this will be a 40–60 minute lesson. In some cases, e.g. growing seeds, the investigation will be spread over several days. The objective is that they will write as they work. The children need to realise that neatness and spelling at this stage are not the priority (they will be later on). They need to see the computer as something that you can **spend a few minutes 'thinking' on, rather than spending long periods writing out large chunks of text.**

I Used Information Technology in My Science Investigation

name

My science investigation was about . . .

I found out that . . .

I used the computer to . . .

The computer was useful because . . .

Fig. 10.5. Proforma for children's evaluation of the use of IT in science

This activity will reveal many considerations required when such practical work is associated with computers:

- access;
- number of children on the computer at a time;
- proximity to the practical work;
- time;
- teacher involvement.

We have provided a proforma for children to evaluate the use of computers (Figure 10.5). You might want to repeat the use of this with other children, different software and different investigations.

You will need to make your own evaluation. You might consider:

(a) things which affect the science, and

(b) practicalities in the classroom.

If you can repeat this exercise you may find different software and different experiments are more suited to science. It might be interesting to glance at the Programme of Study for Science and for IT to see how many aspects of the National Curriculum you are covering.

### Activity 3 – Talking to other co-ordinators and the senior management team
(Time required: 2 hours)
ICT is cross-curricular – as a classteacher you ought to speak to both the ICT and science co-ordinator as well as keeping the senior management aware of what you are doing. Science co-ordinators should speak to the ICT co-ordinator and others, as well as a member of the senior management team. Often this will mean a meeting with the headteacher.

Such meetings are unlikely to occur all at once. They could be part of your short- and medium-term action planning for the weeks and term ahead. But what will you talk about? It is easy to become diverted when talking about ICT as it is such a large area. Money (or the lack of it) can often appear to get in the way.

First decide the objective of such a meeting. Is it to:

```
┌─────────────────────────────────────────────────────────────┐
│ Agenda for Meeting With....                                  │
│ ┌──────────────────────────┬──────────────────────────────┐ │
│ │  agenda                  │  notes                       │ │
│ │                          │                              │ │
│ │                          │                              │ │
│ │                          │                              │ │
│ │                          │                              │ │
│ ├──────────────────────────┴──────────────────────────────┤ │
│ │              action points                               │ │
│ │  what?              who?              when?              │ │
│ │                                                          │ │
│ │                                                          │ │
│ │                                                          │ │
│ └──────────────────────────────────────────────────────────┘ │
└─────────────────────────────────────────────────────────────┘
```

Fig. 10.6. Agenda proforma

- let them know what you are doing?

- involve them by seeking advice?

- get them on your side?

Construct a simple agenda (see Figure 10.6). Remember to make room to allow them to contribute. Science may be your area but you are interested in their views. This will be a two-way process.

The agenda might include:

- you describing your aims;

- them commenting on this;

- your explanation of how this fits into your overall aim for science;

138

- you asking them if they are aware of such work in or outside school;

- some consideration of how this affects their responsibility area;

- a discussion of ways forward.

You should always sum up at the end of such meetings and determine a number of action points. Be clear about who will do what and how the others will know it has been done. Be aware that you may be stepping on to a colleague's territory. It is worth being sensitive to such professional concerns.

## RESOURCE-BASED SCIENCE

Now we turn our attention back to the science and to a different aspect of IT in science, that is, resource-based IT activity. Here we have in mind software or applications which contain science content. Some examples are listed in Figure 10.7.

For many teachers the availability of such software will be limited. It will be worth spending a little time talking to colleagues about programs they have used and what software is available in school. Other co-ordinators should be able to assist. Going further afield to local teachers centres, SEMERC, etc may give you the opportunity to see software but only rarely to borrow software. Software companies often provide free demonstration discs. However, you would be well advised to approach a local advisory teacher or consultant who will be able to make specific recommendations about your needs.

### Activity 4 – IT resource-based science: evaluating potential
(Time required: 1 hour)
First you will need to select an item of software which contains scientific content. These questions may assist you in selecting software for this task. Does the software:

- address any elements of the content in the science PoS?

- encourage aspects of investigation (Sc. 1)?

- stimulate questions?

In a large program like *Science Explorer* which takes hours to work through, you may wish to focus on one section of the program. Use the format in Figure 10.8 for your evaluation.

139

| Supplier and age range | Brief description | Science element |
|---|---|---|
| *Plantwise*<br><br>Upper KS2 | An interactive science database which is accessed by menus and windows on the screen and which includes graphics, some animation and sound and test explanations of the science of plants. | Children may reinforce ideas and be introduced to new ideas. Can lead to other investigations, e.g. what are the effects of light on plants? |
| *P.B. Bear's Birthday Party*<br><br>KS1 | A truly interactive CD ROM for all those learning to and who can read. A series of games include animation and sound in classification, observation, etc of clothes, materials, energy, food, sound, etc. | Lots of starting points for science! |
| *Crystal Rainforest*<br>KS2 | An adventure simulation program which has a strong environmental content and which focuses on orientation skills. | Contains a number of Logo type activities. |
| *Badger Trails*<br>KS2 | This simulation takes us to a badger set and allows us to see aspects of the lives of badgers. | A strong environmental theme. Good for processes of life. |
| *My World*<br><br>KS1 and 2 | This software forms a platform for a huge selection of resource-based items. Examples which could be used in science include: minibeasts, life cycles, etc. | Range through recognition to classification. Often suitable for younger children. |

| | | |
|---|---|---|
| *Science explorer* KS2 | Encyclopaedia-style CD ROM with accessible information and investigations to enhance science classrooms. | Starting points, research and extensions to other learning in science. |
| *Garden Wildlife* KS2 | A simulation of a garden which children explore. | Starting points for scientific study of a garden environment with a range of activities. |

Fig. 10.7. Examples of resource-based science

The proof of the pudding is in the eating! So we suggest that you plan to include either this item of software or another in a future piece of classroom science. If the software is new to the children you might like to introduce it to them by:

- having short (5–10 minute), whole-class, 'together' sessions when you look at the software, i.e. its introductory screens and menus (get as many children up as possible during the demo to type on the keys) and look at new aspects;

- training two, three or four children to use the program who then train and/or assist other children (this will not replace you but will assist you);

- providing some simple instructions or reminders on cards or posters around the computer;

- asking children who have had some time on the software to report back to the class on developments.

It is always a good idea to ensure that children know how to locate, load, save and print files (it is not uncommon for children in Reception to do these things).

Name of software ................... Type of software ...................

Brief summary of the activity within the software ...........................

| Starting points | How could I develop science in my classroom from here? |
| --- | --- |
| Investigative science | |
| Scientific content | |

Fig. 10.8. Evaluating the potential of software for science

## Activity 5 – Evaluating the use of educational software
(Time required: 1 hour)

Such evaluation is essential as the use of ICT is expensive in terms of equipment, your time and of course the children's time. Here we suggest that you select one or both of the proformas in Figure 10.8 which might form the basis of evaluation. The first one might be conducted once over a 10–15 minute period or conducted for 3–5 minutes and repeated several times.

Using the suggestions in Figure 10.9 will give you concrete evidence. This can be added to your day-to-day observations and impressions as well as review by the children (see Figure 10.5). It is important to remember that whilst an application may be deemed of little value to a whole class or school, there may be individual children who will benefit from it greatly.

You need to form judgments about the following questions related to the application:

- How did science benefit from the use of this application?

- Are some children benefiting more than others?

- How might I improve the use of this application in the future?

| IT Observation Schedule | | | | Diary of Application Use | |
|---|---|---|---|---|---|
| Software or application ................... Activity................................. Age range............. Dates........... | | | | Software or application ................... Activity................................. Age range............. Dates ........... | |
| Names | Time | Length of obs. | Are the children being scientific? If so what are they doing? | Date | Observations/reflections |
| | | | | | |

Fig. 10.9. Schedule or diary? Observing children using ICT in science

## USING ICT IN SCIENTIFIC INVESTIGATIONS

It might be helpful for readers of this activity to reacquaint themselves with David Byrne's advice in Book 1 (Bk. 1, Byrne, 8) on the process of investigative science. In this book, Ron Ritchie (Chapter 9) includes a useful self-assessment activity for children.

It is worth reminding ourselves of the words of Phipps (1994) who suggests that children are often not collecting the right kind or even sufficient data to formulate any results. Try to look for opportunities to handle data, to explore patterns and examine relationships.

In Activity 2 above we looked at the contribution which text-handling and word-processing might make to science investigations.

There are opportunities for the use of ICT at each stage of the science process. Here are two examples, one from KS1 and the second from KS2.

## KS1 (Year 2) – How many flowers grow in our school grounds?

This question was posed by a teacher who followed with another question: what do we mean by the word 'flower'? The teacher was not

---

name: Clover
colour of the flower: purple
colour of the leaf: green
place: field
notes: lots of Clover
questions: why do some have 4 leaves?

name: Rose
colour of the flower: yellow
colour of the leaf: green
place: outside the nursery
notes: lots of flowers and thorns
questions: why do they have thorns?

name: Dandelion
colour of the flower: yellow
colour of the leaf: green
place: on the field
notes: there are more Dandelions
questions: why do they only grow on the football pitch?

name: Plantain
colour of the flower: green
colour of the leaf: green
place: grows on the field and the school
questions: how do the bees see the green flower?

name: Rose Bay Willow Herb
colour of the flower: pink
colour of the leaf: green
place: in the wild area and by the railway
notes: taller than Emma, 140 cm

---

Fig. 10.10. File 'Flowers' from database

expecting a scientific definition but was pleased by the collective response which was recorded on a poster. The class followed this discussion with a short walk outside. They examined plants which were in flower. The children were not puzzled by the plants which were not in flower at that time. They explained that these plants were 'too young', 'they're the babies!' Some children claimed that these plants were flowering 'in my garden'. Several children had difficulty with examples like clover and the grasses. An overheard conversation included 'they are flowers but not like real flowers!'

The teacher then introduced these children to a flatfile database containing half a dozen files each of which described a plant on the school site. She introduced this to the class as a group. The children were allowed to browse it. She supplied examples of the leaf and flower (where possible) of each plant beside the computer so that the children could move freely from plant material to database. One child suggested a change to the file because the file said that the daisy flower was yellow and white. The child had spotted flecks of pink. These were also found on the daises outside and so this detail was added. The next step was to add a new file. The teacher met the children on

| | test | Asda | Tesco | Kwik S | Co-op |
|---|---|---|---|---|---|
| 1 | test | Asda | Tesco | Kwik S | Co-op |
| 2 | 1 | 350 | 380 | 410 | 410 |
| 3 | 2 | 390 | 360 | 350 | 420 |
| 4 | 3 | 400 | 360 | 340 | 380 |
| 5 | 4 | 390 | 350 | 390 | 410 |
| 6 | 5 | 400 | 370 | 410 | 420 |
| 7 | 6 | 400 | 340 | 400 | 430 |
| 8 | 7 | 390 | 370 | 370 | 490 |
| 9 | 8 | 390 | 380 | 380 | 470 |
| 10 | 9 | 380 | 370 | 390 | 400 |
| 11 | 10 | 390 | 380 | 390 | 420 |
| 12 | 11 | 400 | 380 | 390 | 420 |
| 13 | 12 | 400 | 380 | 410 | 430 |
| 14 | 13 | 390 | 360 | 370 | 430 |
| 15 | 14 | 390 | 360 | 420 | 420 |
| 16 | 15 | 380 | 350 | 390 | 450 |
| 17 | total | 5840 | 5410 | 5810 | 5950 |
| 18 | | | | | |

Fig. 10.11. 'Bags' spreadsheet

the yard at the end of playtime. The teacher selected a flower they did not have. The class then returned to the classroom to sit together and complete a poster which was a copy of the computer screen. Two children then typed in the details. This process was repeated two or three times with different children adding files. The work proceeded as an ICT strand to the science which encouraged careful observation and recording. (See Figure 10.10.)

## KS2 (Year 5) – Supermarket bags

When a group of children examined the strength of various shopping bags they were faced with a number of problems once they had established the question, 'Which plastic shopping bag is the best?' First they had to decide what they meant by best! Strongest? Largest carrying capacity? Most attractive? The children felt that strength was the thing that they were interested in. They then needed a fair test for strength. They tried a number of options including: trying to overload the bag with weights (the bags proved to be too strong for the weights available, plus this appeared dangerous); they tried rubbing the plastic with sandpaper (this was rejected as the children felt it was not realistic); plus other options. After some time they cut and labelled thin strips of the plastic so that they could test the strength of the plastic materials. They then started testing but found that different experiments got different results. Their teacher suggested that this might be because they were doing things a little differently (that it was not a fair test) and that their sample size was very small. They agreed that samples would be cut more carefully to agreed sizes (previous work on fair testing assisted here) and that they would test fifteen samples of each material. This was the point at which the teacher introduced them to a simple spreadsheet, prepared by the teacher. It dealt with one material at a time, so they used several copies of the same spreadsheet to deal with each bag. The children were delighted to see that the spreadsheet would do the maths for them. Most of these children were happy with the idea of an average. The decimal points had to be ignored by some children in the class but a number had recently started work on decimals and were delighted to see 'real' decimals! (See Figure 10.11.)

The examples above include a flatfile database and a spreadsheet. As well as the text-handling seen earlier, we are able to use ICT for sensing and control. The example in Figure 10.12 summarises an investigation using a palmtop computer, connected to an interface (a separate box which in this case processes information) which allows

Items of Clothing
Which material is the best insulator?
Which material keeps your hand warmest?
Can you devise a fair test to compare gloves? socks?

If you simply put the thermometer into the glove what will the results tell you?
What could you add to make it more useful?

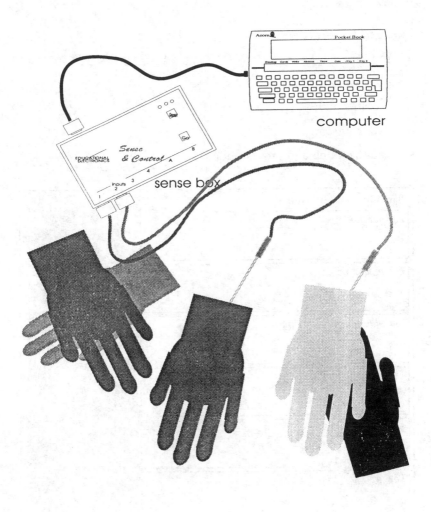

Fig. 10.12. Datalogging 'Gloves'

147

children to sense temperature and determine which material provides the most thermal insulation.

## Activity 6 – Scientific investigations
(Time required: 1 hour)
Use the proforma in Figure 10.13 to examine the potential for all aspects of IT in one or more scientific activities. Look for opportunity to develop:

● question formation:

● prediction;

● observation;

● classification;

● data gathering;

● data handling and presentation;

Planning an Investigation

*our question*

*our prediction*

*our plan for our experiment*

*our evidence*

*so our conclusion is . . .*

*now we know that . . .*

Note possible use of Information Technology

Fig. 10.13. Potential for science in a practical investigation

- considering evidence;
- communication.

In Book 1 we examined the broad categories of IT applications:

- communication;
- data handling;
- modelling;
- monitoring and sensing;
- control.

## PROGRESSION IN THE USE OF ICT IN SCIENCE

Progression in the use of ICT in science can be achieved in a number of ways (see Figure 10.14). Book 1 explained that databases can be used in a number of ways and that they can be used progressively. Particular items of software can be easily configurable so that they can be made suitable for younger or less experienced children. *Pendown* is an example where text-handling tools can be removed from the tool bar to avoid complication. Applications like *Datasweet* which contain a set of several databases can provide for some progression within the set. The computer itself is configurable – the

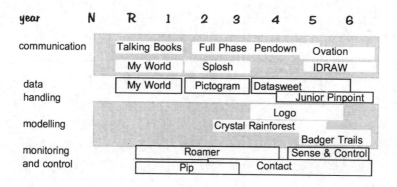

Fig. 10.14. Selection of software to achieve progression

149

mouse can be slowed down. Software (*Minimouser*) will inactivate the MENU and SELECT mouse buttons on the Acorn computers, thus removing difficulty for some children.

## Activity 8 – Mapping progression of IT in science in your school

(Time required: 2 hours)

By examining your curriculum plan alongside the National Curriculum IT Programme of Study, you or your colleagues should be able to fill in the two left-hand columns of Figure 10.15. What goes in the third column will depend on your policy of suggesting or prescribing activities. In order for this activity to contribute we would suggest that it ought to contain activities likely to be used to deliver the science in that year. Thus decisions about software in the final column will be driven by three factors:

| | Programmes of Study | Learning Objective | Activity | Software |
|---|---|---|---|---|
| Reception | | | | |
| Year 1 | | | | |
| Year 2 | | | | |
| Year 3 | | | | |
| Year 4 | | | | |
| Year 5 | | | | |
| Year 6 | | | | |

Fig. 10.15. Mapping progression in IT within science through a primary school (Adapted from *The Bolton LEA Scheme of Work for IT*, Bolton Metropolitan Council, 1997)

- Which software is available?

- Which software is most suitable?

- Which software will build on the children's previous science and ICT experience?

We consider the first question important but of least educational value!

## CONCLUSION

The most important thing is to make a start. Find some software, explore it and develop your own confidence. Choose an application that is straightforward to use but which contributes to the children's science. Science is an excellent starting point for word processing, handling data, modelling and monitoring. Children will become confident very quickly if they are given the opportunity to learn.

Once you gain confidence promote this use of computers by involving colleagues. Engage senior members of staff in supporting you as you explore different areas of ICT use in science. Remember the importance of supportive approaches: some colleagues may be very anxious about ICT.

If you are or hope to be a curriculum manager for science you will need to be aware of the need to write ICT into the science policy. You will need to be clear about how you mean to deliver ICT in science. Peet (Bk. 1, Peet, 13) provides good advice on policy-writing.

IT can positively enhance science. It assists children just as it assists 'scientists'. You will need to place considerable emphasis on using the right software and using it well. ICT is an expensive resource. However, ICT is powerful, exciting, challenging and it can be scientific.

## SOFTWARE MENTIONED

(Most available in Archimedes and PC and in other formats)

| | |
|---|---|
| Garden Wildlife | Anglia Multimedia |
| My World, Pages | Northwest SEMERC |
| Science Explorer | YITM/SEMERC |
| Pictogram, Datasweet II, Retreeval | Kudlian |
| Clicker | Crick Computing |
| KidPix | ESM/Tag |
| Badger Trails, Plantwise | Sherston Software |
| Crystal Rainforest | Sherston Software |

| | |
|---|---|
| Talking Books (various) | Sherston Software |
| Contact | NCET |
| Usbourne Explorer | Main Multimedia |
| P.B. Bears' Birthday, Encyclopaedia of Science, The Ultimate Human Body | Dorling Kindersley |
| Roamer | Valiant Technology |
| PIP | Swallow Systems |
| Sense and Control | Educational Electronics |
| Minimouser | Resource |
| Picture Point, Junior Pinpoint | Longman Logotron |
| Counter, First Workshop, Number Box | Black Cat |

## USEFUL ADDRESSES

Anglia Multimedia, PO Box 18, Benfleet, Essex SS7 1AZ. Tel: (01268) 755811. Email: anglian@aol.com

Association for Science Education (ASE), College Lane, Hatfield, Hertfordshire. Tel: (01707) 267411. Fax: (01707) 266532. Internet: http://www.ase.org.uk/

British Educational Communication Technology Agency (BECTa), Milburn Hill Road, Science Park, Coventry CV4 7JJ. Tel: (01203) 416994. Fax: (01203) 411418. Internet: http://www.becta.org.uk (previously National Council for Educational Technology – NCET)

Bolton Curriculum IT Centre, Castle Hill Centre, Castleton Street, Bolton, BL2 2JN. Tel: (01204) 366497. Email: boltonteachit@dial.pipex.com

Crick Computing, 1 The Avenue, Spinney Hill, Northampton NN3 6BA. Tel: (01604) 671691. Fax: (01604) 671692. Email: crickcomputing@cix.compulink.co.uk

Data Harvest Group, Educational Electronics, Woburn, Waterloo Road, Leighton Buzzard, Beds. Tel: (01525) 373666. Fax: (01525) 851638. Email: sales@dharvest.demon.co.uk

Dorling Kindersley Multimedia, UK Sales, 9 Hennetta Street, London WC2E 8PS. Tel: (0171) 8365411. Fax: (0171) 8367570. Internet: http://www.dk.com

Educational Electronics, Data Harvest Group Ltd, Woburn Lodge, Waterloo Road, Linslade, Leighton Buzzard, Bedfordshire LU7 7NR. Tel: (01525) 373666. Fax: (01525) 851638. Email: sales@Dharvest demon.co.uk

ESM, Living and Learning Ltd, Duke Street, Wisbech, Cambridgeshire PE13 2AE.

Kudlian Software, 8 Barrow Road, Kenilworth, Warwickshire CV8 1EH. Tel: (01926) 842544

Logotron Ltd, 124 Cambridge Science Park, Cambridge CB4 9ZS. Tel: (01223) 425558. Email: info@logo.com. Internet: http://www.logo.com

Main Multimedia, City House, 16 City Road, Winchester, Hampshire, SO23 8SD. Tel:

Northwest SEMERC, 1 Broadbent Road, Watersheddings, Oldham OL1 4LB. Tel: (0161) 627 446. Fax: (0161) 627 2381. Email: info@semerc.demon.co.uk

Resource, 51 High Street, Keyworth, Derby DE74 2DA.

Sherston Software, Angel House, Sherston, Malmsbury, Wiltshire SN16 0LH. Tel: (01666) 840433. Fax: (01666) 840048. Email: info@sherston.co.uk. Internet: http://www.sherston.com

Swallow Systems, 134 Cock Lane, High Wycombe, Buckinghamshire HP13 7EA. Tel: (01494) 813471

Tag Developments, 25 Pelham Road, Gravesend, Kent DA11 0HU. Tel: (01474) 357350

Topologika, Walside House, Falmouth Road, Penryn, Cornwall TR10 8BE. Tel: (01326) 377771. Fax: (01326) 376755. Email: sales@topolgka.demon.co.uk. Internet: http://www.topolgka

Valiant Technology Ltd, 3 Grange Mill, Weir Road, London SW12 0NE. Tel: (0181) 673 2233. Fax: (0181) 673 6333.

# BIBLIOGRAPHY

Phipps, R. (1994) Data handling in scientific investigations in the primary school, *Education 3–13*, Vol. 22, no. 2, pp. 26–33.

BMBC (1997) *The Bolton LEA Scheme of Work for IT*, Bolton.

# 11
# Cross-Curricular Links in Science

*Carole Naylor and Anthony Pickford*

## INTRODUCTION

The shift away from project-based work in the primary school, towards more subject-centred teaching, has meant that primary teachers, for whom a topic-based approach has worked well in the past, now feel a need to reconsider some of the basic ideas that underpin their practice.

In the complementary volume (Bk. 1, Naylor and Pickford, 11) we looked afresh at how the making of cross-curricular links can benefit teaching and learning. We proposed that links can profitably be made in terms of procedure as well as knowledge interactions. We suggested that investigative work in several curriculum areas requires that evidence be collected and interpreted and conclusions drawn which are based on that evidence.

The following activities are designed to give teachers opportunities to explore the links between curriculum areas in terms of both procedure and content. In Book 1 we gave examples of how these links could be forged at three levels in the primary age phase. The activities below are at teachers' own level but the work on the Foxton Lift could clearly be adapted for use with Key Stage 2 children.

## LOOKING FOR COMMON GROUND

Clearly there are differences in the procedures involved in developing work in science and other curriculum areas. In Activity 1 we consider the proposition that, at the primary level at least, the similarities are sufficiently pronounced for practice in one curriculum area to support and reinforce ways of proceeding in others.

## Activity 1 – Looking for common ground

(Time required: 30 minutes)

(a) The statements in Figure 11.1 are extracts from the National Curriculum Programmes of Study for the curriculum areas indicated below.

---

**Asking Questions:**
A ask questions, e.g. 'How?', 'Why?', 'What would happen if?'
B ask questions including 'What would happen if?' and 'Why?'
C to ask and answer questions, and to select and record information relevant to . . .
D observe and ask questions about . . . features and issues

**Making Predictions**
E that making predictions can be useful in planning what to do
F recognise simple patterns and relationships and make related predictions about them
G predicting outcomes and discussing possibilities

**Planning How to Proceed**
H clarify their ideas through discussion
I use focused exploration and investigation to acquire . . . knowledge, understanding and skills
J develop a clear idea of what has to be done, proposing a sequence of actions, and suggesting alternative methods of proceeding if things go wrong

**Gathering Evidence**
K collect and record evidence to answer the question
L that changing one factor and observing or measuring the effect, whilst keeping other factors the same, allows a fair test or comparison to be made
M access and collect data through undertaking purposeful enquiries

**Interpreting Evidence**
N develop the ability to recognise patterns and to apply their knowledge and understanding to explain them
O search for patterns in their results

---

Fig. 11.1 Statements for Activities 1 and 2

**P** to indicate whether the evidence collected supports any prediction made

**Q** to identify and give reasons for different ways in which . . . is represented and interpreted

**Drawing Conclusions**

**R** to use results to draw conclusions

**S** analyse the evidence, draw conclusions and communicate findings

**T** make general statements of their own, based on evidence they have produced

**Communicating Findings**

**U** reporting and describing events and observations

**V** to communicate what happened during their work

**W** pupils should be given opportunities to observe, question and record and to communicate ideas and information

**X** present information and results clearly, and explain the reasons for their choice of presentation.

Fig. 11.1. continued.

(b) Sort the statements into the subject areas you think they come from – English, Mathematics, Science, Design and Technology, History or Geography.

(c) Check with the answers in Figure 11.2.

## CONSIDERING DIFFERENCES

Having identified common ground in Activity 1, we now examine differences between the statements taken from the Science, History, Geography and Mathematics National Curriculum documents. We wish to consider whether perceived differences are solely based on different content or whether the processes involved in gathering and interpreting evidence are fundamentally different.

**Asking Questions:**

| | |
|---|---|
| A | Science KS1<br>1a Systematic Enquiry |
| B | Mathematics KS1<br>Using and Applying Mathematics<br>4b |
| C | History KS2<br>Key Elements 4b |
| D | Geography KS2<br>2a |

**Interpreting Evidence**

| | |
|---|---|
| N | Geography KS2<br>1c |
| O | Mathematics KS2<br>Using and Applying Mathematics<br>4b |
| P | Science KS1 & 2<br>AT1 3e AT1 3d |
| Q | History KS2<br>Key Elements 3a |

**Making Predictions**

| | |
|---|---|
| E | Science KS2<br>AT1 1b |
| F | Mathematics KS1<br>Using and Applying Mathematics<br>4b |
| G | English KS1<br>Speaking and Listening<br>1a |

**Drawing Conclusions**

| | |
|---|---|
| R | Science KS1 & 2<br>AT1 3d AT1 3c |
| S | Geography KS2<br>2c |
| T | Mathematics KS2<br>Using and Applying Mathematics<br>4c |

**Planning How to Proceed**

| | |
|---|---|
| H | Design & Technology<br>KS1 3b |
| I | Science KS1<br>Systematic Enquiry 1b |
| J | Design & Technology<br>KS2 3f |

**Communicating Findings**

| | |
|---|---|
| U | English KS2<br>Speaking & Listening<br>1a |
| V | Science KS1<br>AT1 3a |
| W | Geography KS1<br>2 |
| X | Mathematics KS2<br>Using and Applying Mathematics<br>3c |

**Gathering Evidence**

| | |
|---|---|
| K | Geography KS2 2b |
| L | Science KS2<br>AT1 1d |
| M | Mathematics KS2<br>Handling Data 1b |

Fig. 11.2. Answers for Activities 1 and 2

Fig.11.3. Foxton Boat Lift

## Activity 2 – Considering differences

(Time required: 20 minutes)
(a) Consider the statements under the headings:
Gathering Evidence
Interpreting Evidence
Drawing Conclusions

(b) Discuss what is is that makes an investigation scientific, historical, geographical, etc. Is it simply that the investigations are concerned with different subject matter or are there more fundamental differences?

## CROSS-CURRICULAR INTERACTIONS

The making of cross-curricular links is also important at the level of content. In some contexts, elements of knowledge from different curriculum areas must interact, within the learning process, if understanding is to develop. The tasks that follow are based on an example which shows clearly the fundamental and sometimes complex nature of knowledge interactions.

Activities 3 and 4 make use of the photograph of Foxton Boat Lift in Figure 11.3. The intention of the two tasks is to explore how a cross-curricular process of critical evaluation might be used to (a) analyse evidence and (b) plan for investigations. In carrying out the process, knowledge and understandings derived from several subjects will be developed.

## Activity 3 – Looking at evidence: using the process of critical investigation

(Time required: 30 minutes)
Look at the photograph of Foxton Boat Lift (Figure 11.3). In this activity it is important to approach the photograph without pre-conceptions. Take it at face value and use only the content of the picture to facilitate the process.

(a) Consider and note down the evidence that it contains. Make a list of everything that you can see in the photograph. As well as recording larger features, try to note down some smaller details too. Technical vocabulary is not important at this stage, so do not worry about giving everything its correct name. Look at the people in the photograph – where are they and what do they appear to be doing?

(b) How do you interpret the evidence? What does the photograph tell you? Consider what the photograph appears to show. What can you deduce about the Lift and how it worked, about when and where the photograph might have been taken, about the mechanisms employed?

(c) What conclusions about the Lift can be drawn from the photograph? Are you able to make clear statements about its purpose, structure, systems and usage? How do you think it works?

(d) Can an effective cross-curricular investigation be carried out based on this single source?

Even when focused upon one source, the process of investigation will have drawn upon cross-curricular skills, alongside those from specific subject areas, to generate knowledge and understandings. This knowledge will not be in isolated, subject-labelled blocks, but will be linked and interactive. An understanding of the technology of the Lift will be based upon its technological features, such as the pulley wheels or the chimney stack, our scientific understandings and upon historical clues such as people's dress. Although the photograph is a historical primary source, it will have developed understandings across subject boundaries.

## QUESTIONS FOR INVESTIGATION

The next activity is concerned with the generating of questions for investigation. Again the same photograph is used. The intention here is to show how question raising, leading to the planning of investigations, is not a subject-bound activity. It is one that works best if an awareness of the process of critical investigation is uppermost. Possible investigations within specific curriculum areas will be generated, alongside questions that are cross-curricular in nature.

### Activity 4 – Questions for investigation (1)
(Time required: 20 minutes)
Look at the photograph of Foxton Boat Lift again.

(a) This time, instead of analysing and interpreting the evidence in the photograph, consider what the source does not show and what questions are raised.

(b) Make a list or a chart of all the questions that the photograph prompts. Initially, subject areas and the suitability of the questions for investigation should not be a concern.

Once questions have been generated, then it is appropriate to consider:

- their suitability for investigation;

- the curriculum areas within which they fit or to which they apply;

- the process of investigation which might be used – is it a process or a set of investigational skills from within a specific subject area or is it a process that draws from the skills of all or some subject areas?

## Activity 5 – Questions for investigation (2)
(Time required: 20 minutes)

(a) Consider the questions you have raised. The next step in the planning process is to identify those that are suitable for investigation by primary children. These are the key questions.

(b) Once you have done this, identify how the key questions relate to specific subject areas. Group the questions under National Curriculum subject headings; for example, Science, Mathematics, History, Geography, Design and Technology.

(c) Not all the questions will fit neatly within subject boundaries. Finally, identify any key questions which are cross-curricular in nature and would lead to investigations drawing on skills and knowledge from more than one subject.

The final category of questions for investigation is likely to be small, but in many ways, these questions may be the most stimulating and worthwhile. For example, a question such as 'If the Lift is no longer working, then why did it close?' would need to be investigated through mainly historical research. The answers generated would add to knowledge and understandings in the areas of Geography (the location of the Lift), Design and Technology (the limitations of the available technology) and History (changing transport priorities).

## PLANNING FOR SCIENCE WITHIN A CROSS-CURRICULAR CONTEXT

The final task involves the outline planning of investigations, leading from the photograph, within one curriculum area – Science. In planning investigations and experiments, it is still important to recognise and record the possible contributions of skills and knowledge from other curriculum areas. It is at this point in the planning process that an awareness of the commonality between investigational approaches is most important. Meaningful and relevant links can then be made at a procedural level and at the level of knowledge and understanding.

### Activity 6 – Planning for science within a cross-curricular context
(Time required: 30 minutes)

(a) Use your usual planning format to plan, in outline, the activities and investigations in Science that could develop from the photograph.

(b) Record the places in the programme when skills and knowledge from other subjects would be important.

(c) When finished, consider how your outline plan would augment and support similar plans for other curriculum areas.

## CONCLUSION

The photograph of the Foxton Lift offers a starting point which provides the opportunity to explore the technological application of scientific principles. Teachers would have no difficulty in obtaining similar historical photographs of features within their locality, although a visit to an actual site would clearly be more motivating for children. Census material, old maps of the locality, artefacts and stories would also make useful starting points. For primary teachers forging links between content areas presents little difficulty, but in order to make appropriate links at the level of procedure the teacher needs to look at the subjects of the curriculum from a slightly different angle, focusing primarily on the processes through which learning will take place.

## APPENDIX: THE FOXTON BOAT LIFT –
## BACKGROUND INFORMATION

### Geography

Foxton is in Leicestershire, about 14 miles from Leicester and 5 miles from Market Harborough. The site of the Boat Lift is to the south of the village adjacent to Foxton Locks on the Leicester section of the Grand Union (formerly Grand Junction) Canal. Except for the slope, or inclined plane, on which it was built, little evidence now remains of the Lift. Its short life-span in the early years of this century is a testament to changing transport priorities. It was, to a great extent, the last gasp of the canal-building industry in this country before it succumbed to competition from the railways.

At its inception it was a bold scheme – an attempt by the directors of the Grand Junction Company to modernise and speed up their canal carrying operations. The Leicester section was a vital link between their main London to Birmingham route and northern waterways accessed via the River Soar and River Trent. Foxton lay at a strategic point in the network, but was proving to be a severe bottleneck because of the flight of narrow locks that descended the hillside into the village. The Boat Lift was designed to bypass the locks and thus speed traffic, attract trade and also encourage the use of more economic wide boats or barges.

The Lift's short working life and failure illustrates clearly the strength of railway competition at the time. There was no significant increase in trade and barge traffic dwindled rather than grew. In many ways the Grand Junction Company's circumstances are mirrored by the position of our railways, one hundred years later, faced by competition from the road haulage industry. The development of one transport network can be seen to supersede and replace another.

The Foxton Inclined Plane Trust was formed in 1980 to carry out restoration and foster public interest in the Boat Lift site. To an extent, they have been successful in that Foxton now attracts many visitors – most of them day-trippers who come to stroll along the towpaths and watch boats negotiate the steep lock flight. Foxton, with its canal-side pub and shop, reflects very clearly the leisure aspect of the canal industry that is now in favour, at the expense of commercial goods-carrying interests. Like most of Britain's canal system, the Leicester section is now maintained as a cruising waterway for holiday-makers, not as a viable transport link.

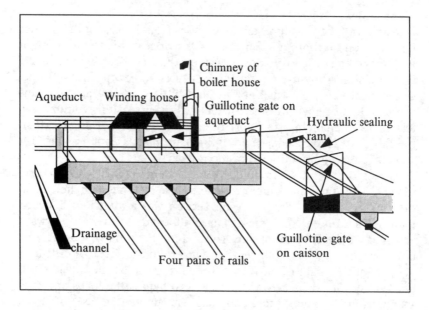

Fig. 11.4. An annotated sketch based on the photograph of Foxton Boat Lift

## History

Work commenced on the Foxton Boat Lift in 1898 under the supervision of the Grand Junction Canal company's chief engineer, Gordon Cale Thomas. Alongside his cousin, Barnabas Thomas, who also helped with the design, his efforts were rewarded by the award of a Gold Medal and Diploma for the Foxton design at the St Louis Exhibition in the USA in 1904. As an engineering achievement, the Lift was a success, but in economic and financial terms it proved to be a miscalculation. Amongst the reasons for the Lift's failure to generate more traffic, the fragmented nature of the canal system appears to have been significant. New customers found it very difficult to calculate through-tolls as each individual canal company had its own rate for its part of a journey – the relatively short passage from Leicester to Birmingham, for example, would involve a boatman in paying varying tolls to five different companies. This situation did not ease until the nationalisation of the canal system in 1945, by which time the Foxton Lift had been dismantled.

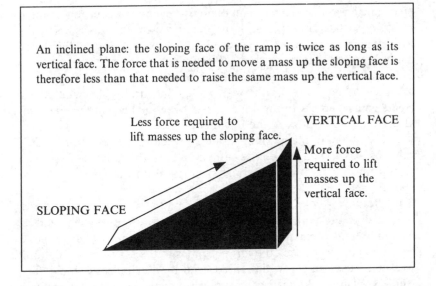

An inclined plane: the sloping face of the ramp is twice as long as its vertical face. The force that is needed to move a mass up the sloping face is therefore less than that needed to raise the same mass up the vertical face.

Less force required to lift masses up the sloping face.

VERTICAL FACE

More force required to lift masses up the vertical face.

SLOPING FACE

Fig. 11.5. The principle of the inclined plane

In many ways the designers and builders of the Lift never had its endurance and reliability tested. For long periods in its working life, from 1898 until 1910, it saw few boats and the staff would have had little to do. By 1917, after years of disuse, most of the engineers who had been responsible for building and maintaining the Lift had left the Grand Junction Company and it was decided that too large an outlay would be involved in putting the Lift back into working order. The minutes of the Company record that in March 1917 it was decided that the 'plant and machinery should be disposed of'. Because of fluctuating prices in the scrap market, it took over ten years for the Lift to be sold for scrap – eventually in 1928 a Shropshire company paid just £250 for the rusted remains of the Lift.

## Technology
The Foxton Lift was a product of the age of steam. The mechanisms and systems used reflect clearly the principles and practices of engineering design at the turn of the century (see Figure 11.4). Some

fascinating comparisons and contrasts can be made with the approaches and methods that would be used in a similar context now.

The chimney stack, in the background of the photograph, reveals the source of the Lift's motive power: steam. The main hauling mechanism was driven by a compound two-cylinder steam engine rated at 25 hp with another as backup. Steam power also pressurised the hydraulic system, which was used to raise and lower the Lift's guillotine gates and work the tank sealing rams.

The tanks were lowered and raised on rails, each tank being linked to the winding house, with its huge hauling drums, by wire ropes. Boats gained access to the Lift via narrow aqueducts and canal arms at the top and bottom of the inclined plane.

The problem of maintaining a seal between the canal and the Lift's caissons was solved by the use of hydraulics – the tanks were pushed tightly into place by sealing rams positioned on the slope at the far end of each tank.

Hydraulic pipes to the guillotine gates on the aqueducts were fixed, but those to the tanks had to be attached before their gates could be moved. When a caisson reached the top or bottom of the slope, a guard manually connected hydraulic pipes to the tank-gates. The joint was made using a screw-thread covered by a cylindrical shield. The whole system would have been subject to corrosion and leakage with minimal frost protection being provided by the water and anti-freeze mixture in the pipes. With hindsight, the Lift's mechanisms appear clumsy, cumbersome and highly labour intensive. In many ways, however, this is a false impression as, for its time, the Foxton Boat Lift was an example of advanced engineering practice.

## Science

The scientific principles underpinning the design and operation of the Lift are many. The Lift can be viewed as a sequence of energy transfers – effected by the use of machines such as levers, pulleys and gears – with a central purpose of lifting and lowering a mass.

Central to the design was the principle of the inclined plane (see Figure 11.5), an idea used since ancient times to ease the movement of large masses – the Pyramids were probably constructed using ramps to raise the stone blocks. The ramp on which the Lift was built reduced the effort needed to raise the boats by increasing the distance that they had to move. The Lift, therefore, required a smaller energy input than if the boats had been raised vertically.

The issue of friction would have played a significant part in the Lift's design. Lubrication would have been used at key points in the system to reduce it – for example, in the hauling engine – and at other points friction would have been essential to slow the mechanism down.

The Lift's control mechanisms were predominantly hydraulic. They worked by increasing and transferring force through a fluid from one piston to another. Hydraulic systems take advantage of the fact that a fluid – in the case of the Foxton Lift, it was water mixed with anti-freeze – is very much harder to compress than a gas. Therefore, pressure exerted by a piston at one end of a system will result in an immediate and firm response at the other end. Such an effect can be seen clearly in a simple water-filled system, such as two syringes linked by plastic tubing. A larger system, such as the one at Foxton, would need to be pressurised and the resultant problem of leakage would make it unpredictable and difficult to maintain.

## ACKNOWLEDGMENT

The authors wish to thank British Waterways (Central, Willow Grange, Church Road, Watford, Hertfordshire WD1 3QA) for permission to reproduce the picture of Foxton Lift.

# 12
# Home–School Links

*Alan Cross and Conrad Chapman*

## INTRODUCTION

The importance and relevance of home–school, parent and teacher links in the area of science were recognised by Chapman in Book 1 (Chapter 12) as a fundamental aspect of primary education which seeks to form partnerships with parents. If schools are to involve parents in their child's education then curriculum areas like science offer considerable opportunities. Schools need to be welcoming and encouraging to parents and to develop whole-school policy to further such partnership.

This chapter was written for all those interested in furthering both science and home-school links. We aim to add to the many strategies outlined in Book 1 by providing a framework and concrete assistance to those embarking on home-school links in science. Below you will find a series of suggested steps including activities. The chapter identifies three main areas for action:

- a home–school science liaison review;

- constructing an action plan;

- a first step – a science workshop for parents or others.

## A HOME–SCHOOL LIAISON REVIEW

Your experience in home-school work and that of the school will affect the time spent on the next activity. It is important to find out what has occurred in the past. First we suggest that you look at school documentation and then talk to colleagues, including senior managers, and then parents. A series of key questions is presented which should be addressed by as wide a range of staff and parents as possible.

### Activity 1 – What does school documentation tell you about the school's home–school links (in science)?
(Time required: 1–2 hours)
As you are building up a picture of the parents and possible activities in science, you must find out about your school's approach. If you are very lucky there will be a recently written policy on parental involvement. For the rest it will be a matter of reading documentation and talking to the senior management team and colleagues. (Use Figure 12.1.)

### Activity 2 – Considering key questions
(Time required: 1 hour)
Examine Figure 12.2 and use the same format (shown in Figure 12.3) to note your thoughts. Some areas might be considered as short- or medium-term goals, others for the longer term. Consider all six headings. The important thing is their relevance to your school and to science. These headings would make very useful discussion points with staff.

### Activity 3 – Discuss home–school links in science with the headteacher, teachers and parents
(Time required: 2–3 hours)
To go any further along this road you need the approval and support of the headteacher. Talking to the headteacher will be valuable as primary headteachers control much of the opportunity for home–school liaison. Headteachers, for example, often wish to approve all correspondence going home to parents from teachers. Similar questions will assist discussions with colleagues and parents. The headings from Figure 12.3 may prove useful here.

*Before the meeting*
- Be clear about what you mean by home–school links.

- Be absolutely clear about what you mean by primary science. (You might re-read Chapter 1 in Book 1.)

- Be prepared to state what you are proposing, what range of things might happen.

- Can you say how the children will benefit?

| Documentation | Is parental involvement mentioned | To what extent is it an example of good practice? | Does it relate to science? |
| --- | --- | --- | --- |
| School brochure | | | |
| Policy documents: | | | |
| – maths | | | |
| – English | | | |
| – Foundation subjects, etc. | | | |
| Assessment, reporting and recording | | | |
| Special Needs | | | |
| Behaviour, etc. | | | |
| Letters home | | | |
| Annual report of the governing body | | | |
| Booklet of advice about hearing children read | | | |
| Reading record | | | |
| Others | | | |

Fig. 12.1. Reviewing school documentation

**PARENTS' VIEWS**

Will parents' views and experiences be considered in the planning stage of science activities? If so, how?
How will you assess parental response to science initiatives/activities?

**COMMUNICATING WITH PARENTS**

What strategies do you use to keep parents and the community in touch with school life and science in particular?
*Written communication* – how understandable is it? How readable? Is it well presented? Do parents require translation?
*Verbal communication* – consider, individual/small group/class group/whole school.
*Hidden communication* – buildings, notices, displays.
What methods are used to enable parents to know how their child is getting on in science? e.g. parent/teacher consultation, workshops, reports, profiles, home visits.

**PARENTS' INVOLVEMENT IN THEIR CHILD'S SCIENCE**

How are parents involved and where does it take place?
How does the school share professional expertise in science with parents?
What acknowledgement does the school give to parents' special knowledge about
– their own child?
– science?

**Key questions for schools to consider in seeking to involve parents in school science**

**HOME VISITS?**

Will work in science be supported by home visits?
If so, what will be their purpose?
Frequency?
Effect?

**SCHOOL PHILOSOPHY**

What are your educational reasons for involving parents?
What do you do to show that your school welcomes parental involvement in science?
– visually?
– verbally?
– personally?
How is it that parents get these messages about the school's approach?

**PARENTS' NEEDS/OTHER AGENCY SUPPORT**

What types of informal/formal support is offered to develop parents' own scientific knowledge and development?

How are other agencies involved?
(a) Adult education provision
(b) Other ways.

Fig. 12.2. Key questions when considering parental involvement in science

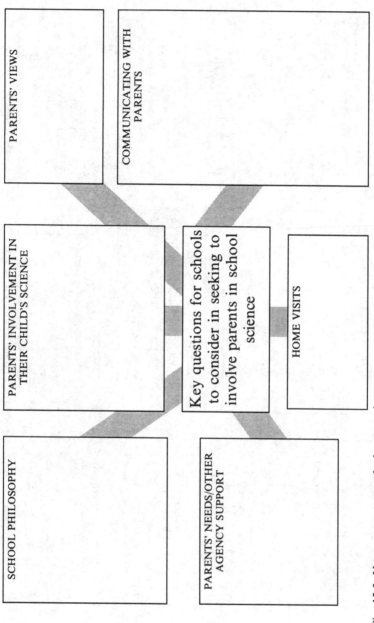

Fig. 12.3. Your responses to the key questions

- Can you say how parents will benefit?

- Can you say how the school will benefit?

## *During the meeting*
- Update the headteacher on developments and thoughts to date.

- Keep the focus on science.

- Establish agreement that home–school links are a 'good thing' and why.

- Establish how this fits into or might complement existing home–school links.

- Consider when all the staff might be involved in discussions.

- Consider how you might include parents as early as possible.

- Consider the role of a review.

- Determine what action is to be taken.

## *After the meeting*
- Start to formalise your plans by constructing an action plan.

- Make sure that all the things you promise to do, happen!

We focus here on the headteacher as this is someone you must get on your side. Similar advice should guide your important discussion with staff colleagues and parents. You should always be aware of your audience. Make yourself aware of their position.

Remember that science itself can be daunting for teachers and parents. We have not all had positive experiences with science. In Book 1, Peet (Chapter 6) and Chapman (Chapter 12) refer to the inequalities faced by some parents and show that for many parents and children science does not always seem accessible. For many, both parents and staff, home–school links present a barrier or at least a challenge. Thus we ought to tread carefully and sensitively.

Access to teaching colleagues can be informal and formal. Access to parents is likely to be informal as fewer opportunities may be available. As such it is always difficult to feel that you have spoken to a representative sample. A questionnaire may assist. You may have to be satisfied with as wide a sample of opinion as is reasonably possible.

## CONDUCTING AN AUDIT

### Activity 4 – An audit of home–school links in science
(Time required: 3–5 hours)
This audit can be conducted with both teachers and parents. (Before conducting this audit you might like to read part of Chapter 14 which suggests an audit.)

Questions which may assist you in an audit of home–school links include:

- What does the school already do in its work in science and with parents?

- Does work in other subjects with parents relate?

- Are there examples of informal activity or discussions?

- Does the situation vary from early primary years to later primary years?

- How much/what do parents want to know about their child's science?

- How much/what do parents want to know about the science taught in school?

- How could the school do better?

- Is it a matter of: events? communication? reporting? parents' science? documentation? notice? involvement?

## CONSTRUCTING AN ACTION PLAN

### Activity 5 – Begin to construct an action plan
(Time required: 2 hours)
By following the flow chart in Figure 12.4 you may be able to begin to construct an action plan. This might physically occupy one or several pieces of paper. You will need to organise information you have gathered so far and information you may yet gather. A target or series of targets agreed with colleagues will give you considerable direction. These targets will include medium- and short-term goals; for example, to:

- discuss the proposals with the school parent governors;

- hold a staff meeting;

- hold a science open evening/day;
- send home information about science topics.

In your school, which of the above would be short-term objectives?

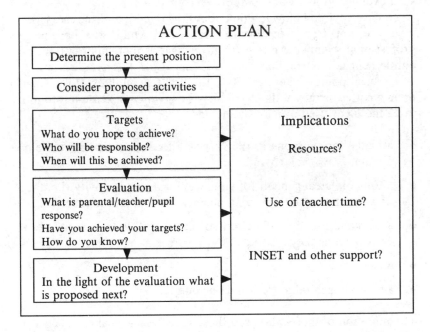

Fig. 12.4. Constructing an action plan

## MAKING A START

Here we offer two alternatives as examples of events that might give you the opportunity to make a start. First we look at the organisation of a workshop for parents (Activity 6) and then a series of activities which children and parents might conduct at home based on a theme (Activity 7).

### Activity 6 – Organising a science workshop for parents

(Time required: 3 hours+)
Consider and make notes on the following advice. What would be the aim of such an event? Talk it over with a colleague and ultimately a senior manager in the school.

## A science workshop – some considerations

Very valuable to you at this stage will be the experience of colleagues who have run similiar events or any events involving parents. Just asking for advice often results in offers of support that might not otherwise be forthcoming. The headteacher will have experience of such events and will want to approve your plans.

You are advised below to think about the overall aim and messages. You are not trying to ensure that every child will become a professional scientist. An important message is that children have an entitlement to science, that science is for all.

A crucial point of these events is the first few minutes. If you hand them a coffee as they walk in you may be giving an excuse not to join in. Some ideas used previously include:

- a badge for everyone as they arrive allocating them to a table or a team;

- a tombola arrangement for similar allocation to activity (i.e. they draw a number and go to an activity bearing that number);

- a personal user-friendly chart so that they colour in a picture of each table as they visit it;

- a challenge;

- a clue at each table for a quiz or puzzle.

The intention of those who used these ideas was to make the event a little different and to encourage parents to relax.

Most events have a short session where the head, the co-ordinator or an invited speaker will talk for a few minutes (no more) about science in the school.

Choose the activities carefully, for ease of involvement and not too messy. Some emphasis on process skills would help you get across important messages.

### Checklist

As you begin to plan for a science workshop for parents, consider the following:

*Intentions*:
- Why are you doing this?  – for science? school?
  home–school links?

- Is this event part of your overall strategy for science?
  – part of your action plan?
- What are the main messages to get over?
  – science for all? partnership? the process of science?
- Date, timing and duration?
  – avoid popular soap opera? will parents be able to get sitters for younger children?

*Nature of the event*:
- Will working parents be able to attend?
  – timing? alternative?
- What is the ideal group size?
  – overall? in groups?
- Where will you hold this event?
  – hall? alternatives?
- What sort of atmosphere are you trying to create?
  – warm? inviting? involvement?
- Will children be invited? If so how will you stop them taking over the activities, whilst some parents opt out?
  – selected children to introduce activities? school children? very young children? crèche?
- Will you give parents certificates or badges?
- Will you have a science theme as in Figure 12.5 or have a little science from each class, or . . .
  – parents need to see the relevance to their children.

*Ensuring access:*
- Will you attract the largest audience?
  – optimum audience? notices? adverts?
- Who will invite the school governors?
- Will language be a problem for some parents?
  – how will these parents get to know? at the event? translation?
- Will you organise a crèche?
  – who? where? sign in/out?
- How will you advertise the event?
  – letter? posters? other events?
- How will you encourage reluctant parents to join in? Put them in pairs?
  – make it sound attractive? ensure similar events go down well!

- Will you have children at each table to introduce the activity?

– can work well, best to train the children to work with adults, the children must not do the science for them!

- Is access to the building clearly marked?

- Make sure you have drinks available (towards the end)

– think about timing here: drinks at the start can slow things down but do create a welcoming atmosphere.

*Organisational matters:*

- How will parents let you know that they are coming?

– a return slip with numbers? tickets?

- Will you have children's work displayed around the room?

– an excellent idea: can you tie in the school plan for display?

- Who will introduce the session? Conclude the session?

– you? the head? a parent? an invited speaker? a video?

- How will you encourage movement around the room?

– ring a bell? ask two members of staff/governors to assist?

*Follow up:*

- Evaluation

– what did parents, colleagues, children, you think? questionnaire?

- Publicity

– take photographs? local press?
– mention in school newsletter?
– report to governors? invite local adviser? secondary school-teachers?

- Review the effect of this event on your future plans for science

- Keep records of the event as evidence of this initiative

These events take very considerable organisation. Do not be too adventurous, but afraid either, as even poorly attended workshops have been considered very successful.

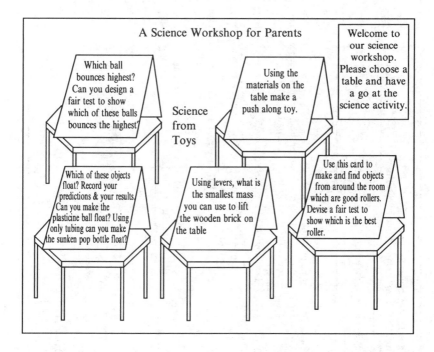

Fig. 12.5. Possible activities in a short science workshop for parents

## Activity 7 – Home–school science activities: activities based around the chapati (Figure 12.6)

(Preparation time required: 1–2 hours)

Can you see opportunities for conducting science activity (wholly or partly) at home? We would suggest that as you are already planning science for the year you build such activity around topics and themes that you are already doing, for example:

| Topic | Home–school activity |
|---|---|
| Ourselves | Find clothes/photos which show how children grow |
| Forces | Draw simple machines in the kitchen, discuss how they work |
| Plants | Observe a sprouting bean (supplied by school) on a daily basis (warn parents about the dangers of seeds and young children, *Be Safe!* ASE, 1990) |

179

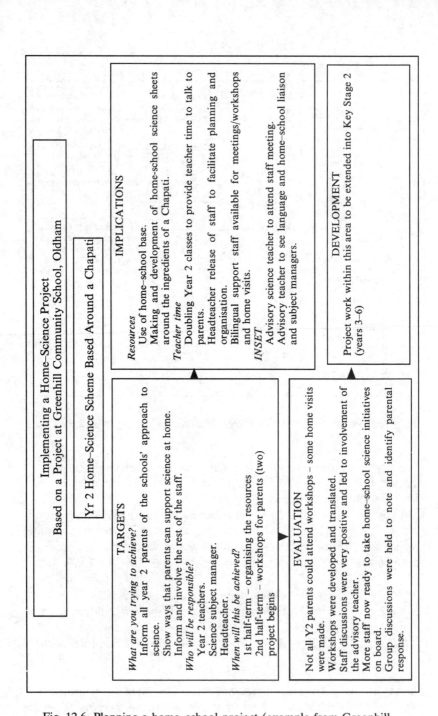

Fig. 12.6. Planning a home–school project (example from Greenhill School, Oldham)

You will find other examples in the SHIPS material (Solomon and Lee, 1991).

Other possible activities include:

- suggestions for holiday science;

- information to parents about a science topic;

- a joint visit to a nature reserve;

- a whole community science investigation, e.g. how many ponds do we have locally? what kinds of birds do we have in the area?

- a speaker;

- a visit to the secondary school;

- a science week, day;

- a competition.

It will be important to review the success of any such activities. Ask for comments from parents and from the staff and children who were present. If you were clear about your aims for the event, evaluation may be more straightforward. Do look for unexpected spinoffs. Be prepared to submit a short report to the headteacher and that such a report may go to the governors.

## CONCLUSION

Parents are interested in their children. However, they often focus their attention on 'the basics' – perhaps we need to convince them that science is a 'basic'? Science is an excellent medium for promoting home-school links where children's achievement in science stands to gain. Presently science represents something that for most parents hardly featured in their own primary education. If schools want a vehicle to say to parents 'look what we are doing, look how good it is and how your children respond to it!' what better vehicle is there than science? For science, parental support is important. In times of pressure on education there has been a tendency to reduce the amount of science taught in primary schools. The long-term future and strength of science may be improved in primary children's education if parents see it as worthwhile and value it.

By now, having read this far you have started along a road which will contribute to your professional development. The topic is science as it contributes to the relationship of your school with the community it serves.

## BIBLIOGRAPHY

Association of Science Education (1990) *Be Safe!* Hatfield: ASE.
Solomon, J. and Lee, J. (1991) *School Home Investigations in Primary Science (SHIPS)*, Hatfield: ASE.

# 13
# The Role of the Science Co-ordinator

*Gill Peet*

## INTRODUCTION

This book and its companion volume are devoted to aspects of the teaching of science as part of primary education. Therefore, most of their content relates directly to the role of the co-ordinator. As a science co-ordinator you will no doubt be selective when considering the relevance of activities to your school. In the companion volume (Bk. 1, Peet, 13) advice was offered in relation to resources and other aspects of the role, such as writing a policy document. In this chapter the focus is pragmatic and asks that you consider your own skills of interaction and influence with colleagues. To be effective as a co-ordinator you need to establish yourself professionally with your colleagues. You need to assess carefully the needs of your school and then choose the most appropriate methods of dealing with issues. Such methods will involve the need to move colleagues in one direction or another. You will therefore have to achieve the involvement of colleagues and their agreement that change will be in the interests of the children. The activities included in this chapter are designed to help give the co-ordinator a focus for personal reflection on these important professional skills.

## ESTABLISHING YOUR ROLE

Do not lose sight of the fact that your ultimate responsibility is to manage science to ensure that all pupils in your school achieve the highest standards of which they are capable in science. To do this it is important that you establish a role for yourself in school that will enable your work to reach out to and benefit all the children and not just the children in your class. If you are not able to influence colleagues your efforts will not permeate the whole school. It is therefore very important that you first establish good relationships. You may have taught in the school for some time and may consider your colleagues to be close friends, but how well do you know them as teachers? It is important that you can be objective in your role. Are you aware of their strengths and weaknesses in teaching science? Does your relationship allow open and honest self-criticism? It is important that you aim to set up good working relationships with the other staff in the school if you are to ensure a whole-school approach to science.

A clear job description will assist you as you and your colleagues will then be fully aware of the extent of your responsibilities. You will also need to negotiate with your headteacher for time to discuss aspects of teaching science with colleagues and you will almost certainly need to visit other classes. Establish the system for buying resources for your area. Most science co-ordinators find it easier to manage resources, respond to needs and monitor the resources when they are personally responsible for the science budget. It is worth persuading your headteacher to give you this responsibility. A carefully prepared action plan will assist these negotiations.

If you are to be successful in developing a good working relationship with colleagues and getting to know their needs, you will first need to know yourself.

## Activity 1 – How well do you know yourself?
(Time required: 1 hour)
Spend a few minutes considering these questions:

- How well do you know your colleagues?

- Are you able to work with a wide range of people?

- How good are you at influencing people?

- How do you feel that colleagues see you in this role?

- How will you cope with colleagues who obstruct your progress?

- How good a listener are you?

- Can you take criticism?

- How will you deal with conflict?

- How confident are you in science? In subject knowledge? In teaching styles?

Thinking about these issues will not always lead to answers, but if you are able to anticipate areas that might inhibit your role, you can achieve a more positive outcome.

You may think that you know your colleagues well, but try the next exercise.

## Activity 2 – How well do you know your colleagues?
(Time required: 1 hour)
Choose a friend or colleague with whom you are comfortable and state separately whether you believe the following statements are true or false. Your colleague should answer them personally, while you have to decide how your colleague will answer.

1. I enjoy teaching best when the children are doing something active and are getting really involved.

2. I feel very confident when doing science.

3. It doesn't worry me if a pupil asks a question I don't know the answer to.

4. I understand the forces acting on a ball when it is thrown into the air.

5. I can identify the variables in an experiment.

6. I believe that science is a set of facts to be learnt.

7. I believe that pupils learn science best from being told and reading about science and that practical activity helps them remember it.

8. Science is a way of understanding and making sense of the world.

9. I enjoy teaching science.

When you have finished, share your answers. How well did you know your colleague?

This exercise may give you both an opportunity to share concerns. It may also illustrate the range of views that exist amongst the school staff. Don't forget to emphasise the areas where you agreed.

## Activity 3 - How well are you able to listen?
(Time required: 1 hour)
Observe two other people talking. Concentrate on the person who is doing most of the listening and make mental notes on their body language, its use and its effect. Consider these points:

- What is the extent of the eye contact used?

- What messages are they giving in their body language?

- What about their body posture?

- And facial expressions?

What effect did all this have on the speaker?
How much can you remember of the conversation?

Think about the implications of what you have learnt about listening and yourself for future discussions with colleagues. If you are going to develop a good relationship with other members of staff so that all views are contributed and considered, you will need to develop your listening skills.

You or your actions will inevitably be criticised at some time and it is useful to consider how you are going to react. You must ensure that you listen to any criticism carefully as it may be valid. It may also tell us a great deal about those who offer it. Critical remarks from colleagues may be a defence mechanism.

## Activity 4 - How will you handle criticism?
(Time required: 30 minutes)
Think about a time when you were criticised (or felt criticised), and ask yourself the following questions:

- How valid was the critical remark?

- How confident were you about this?

- Was it a criticism of your approach or of school policy?

- Was the critical remark positive or negative?

- What positive outcomes could you see?

It is important to remember that we all misunderstand situations from time to time and make criticisms that are unjustified. Do not let criticism affect your relationships with colleagues or upset you. Nobody can please everybody all of the time. Show that you understand their concerns and that you are listening to them. It is a good idea to acknowledge when you are wrong and then decide whether you are going to have to modify your action and if so, how.

The more that colleagues are consulted about your actions, the more likely it is that people will endeavour to work with you. Colleagues want to feel that their views have been considered but they will not want to be consulted on every minor detail. They will, however, value recognition of their input and like to feel that it has made a difference.

## DECIDING WHAT NEEDS TO BE DONE

Having established relationships and a routine for working with people, your next concern is to assess what needs to be done. To ensure success you will need some sort of action plan. In the companion volume (Bk. 1, Peet, 13) it is suggested that you identify short-, medium- and long-term plans. Goals can only be set when there has been a careful examination of the existing situation in order to identify the particular needs of the staff and the school. A policy of monitoring and evaluation will need to be prepared and then carried out as an ongoing exercise. This is discussed fully in Book 1 (Bk. 1, Cross and Chinn, 14) and in the following chapter. Such an exercise should reveal areas that need development.

Ensuring that there is a whole-school approach to the delivery of the science curriculum through agreed investigational and experimental processes is essential. The achievement of a whole-school approach to science is an important medium- and long-term objective if science teaching in your school is going to be successful. Staff development in science should constantly promote whole-school approaches. It is important but not sufficient that you have had some in-service training and have a clear idea of where you want to go and how you want to do it. Your colleagues also have to feel similarly secure and hopefully have the same vision. Where are you going to start? How are you going to start?

### Activity 5 – How are you going to establish the needs of your colleagues?
(Time required: 1 hour)
Consider the following strategies for use in your school situation:

- questionnaires;
- interviews;
- whole-staff meetings;
- classroom observation.

You might opt for one strategy or a combination.

**Questionnaires** can be very effective if staff will give the necessary time and thought to filling them in. This demands a high degree of co-operation from colleagues and presupposes that colleagues will be fully aware of their own needs. For example, the colleague who has never heard of constructivism is unlikely to ask for in-service training in this area. You will need to think about the individuals in your school, the time they have to fill in a questionnaire and the level of awareness they have of their own needs. A questionnaire is usually completed individually and therefore the person completing it is not able to benefit from considering the suggestions of others.

**Individual interviews** may be more appropriate if you have the time to go and speak to all members of staff. They can be a very valuable source of information because they allow teachers to explore their own personal concerns. Information often emerges which the interviewer would not have thought to ask about in a questionnaire.

**Group discussions** allow teachers to bounce ideas off one another and allow them the space to develop their own thoughts while listening to the views of others. It saves time and you are more likely to achieve a consensus about what staff feel they need and how they would like to achieve this.

**Working alongside** colleagues is only useful if you have the opportunity to reflect together after the lesson. Concerns can then be shared and strengths and weaknesses can begin to be recognised and needs identified. You will need to observe the children's work and consider the classes in which it is done well and the reasons why it might be done less well in others. Try to negotiate access to and examine teachers' planning. Do they have a clear understanding of their aims and objectives for teaching science?

# THE MOST APPROPRIATE METHODS OF DEALING WITH ISSUES

## Activity 6 – Constructing an action plan

(Time required: 2 hours)

In Book 1 (Bk. 1, Peet, 13) it was stated that a positive and realistic approach to planning was to have short-term, medium- and long-term plans for the subject.

1. Start by listing everything that you feel you would like to do if circumstances would allow.

2. Clearly there will be some things that you do not have the resources or the time to do immediately. Complete another list entitled 'short-term plans' which will include all the tasks that can be done quite easily and quickly such as buying simple resources, or rearranging their storage. When these jobs are completed you will feel that you are getting somewhere.

3. Medium-term plans will include those things that require preparation and perhaps discussion and agreement. Examples would include assessment and record-keeping policy, schemes of work, significant resource purchase, etc. (see Bk. 1, Peet, 13 for other headings). These items will most likely have to be included in the school development plan.

4. Long-term plans might include objectives that cannot yet be achieved because staff development would be needed first. Such things might include increasing the use of computers in science. In that case you would also need to go back to the medium plan and include the staff development necessary to achieve the longer-term goal. If your longer-term goal is dependent on financial resources then you will need a financial plan stating what is required, why it is required and the exact cost. You will need to negotiate with the headteacher for this to be considered when writing the school development plan.

## Meeting staff development needs

When you have decided on the areas of staff development needs and agreed a budget with the headteacher, how are you going to meet those needs?

Science differs from other areas of the curriculum in that even today many teachers still feel underqualified to teach science and are lacking in confidence. If this is the situation in your school it may be that whole-school development will be preferable to sending individuals to short sessions on small areas of the curriculum. In a whole-school approach to in-service, staff can share strengths and weaknesses and continue to support each other in managing change in their classrooms. INSET training can be run by yourself using some material from, for example, this book or by an outside agency. If you decide to tackle your own INSET you will need to think about the following.

## Activity 7 – Planning INSET
(Time required: 2–3 hours)
In the same way as you do when preparing lesson plans, decide what your learning targets for the session are and keep these in focus when doing all your planning. Adult learning is in some respects similar to that of children and if you choose appropriate activities teachers can model their own teaching approaches on the ones you use. If teachers are to feel comfortable teaching science they need to enjoy it themselves and experience and understand the processes of science. You therefore need to think about doing science as well as talking about it.

When you have chosen the focus for your INSET, you need to think about practicalities.

- Decide how long the session will be and make sure that people have details of times and place in plenty of time.

- Think in detail about the nature of the activities you are going to offer. You will probably need an ice breaker. Even if staff know each other well it helps them to relax.

- Know the aim for each activity you are using and make sure that your session is coherent.

- Think about the activities that will be carried out. Will they be done in pairs, individuals or whole group?

- Think about how much time should be set aside for each activity. This will help you during the session. Remember, sessions never start quite on time.

- Think about the resources you will need for each activity and make sure that you have them all available beforehand.

- Make sure that you have the audio visual equipment you

require and that there are conveniently placed power points in the room.

- Make sure you have made sufficient copies of handouts and that any overhead transparency sheets can be clearly read at the back of the room.

- Think about how you will want people to arrange themselves around the room. If you want staff to work in small groups don't arrange the chairs so that 6 or 7 can sit around one table.

- Think about how you are going to manage the discussion activities. Give people a clear brief and if necessary remind them of it as they work. Give a set time, say ten or fifteen minutes, and give them a few minutes warning before the time is up.

- Try and get around to each group whilst they are working. It helps to give you a flavour of what they are saying and sometimes you may need to lead them a little in the feedback. If there are many groups thinking about things that need to be shared, it might be a good idea to ask them to write down their thoughts and then for you to take this away, collate the information and then return it to the whole group on the next occasion when you meet. This saves time on repetitive feedback and can give colleagues the time to think about the views of others before making decisions on them.

- Always make sure you have thought about your first few sentences and be prepared to be flexible in your timing so that the pace is right for the group. Remember that it is important that your colleagues are given the opportunities to share ideas in a way that they are not normally given the opportunity to do during the school day.

## Ensuring action

At the end of any meeting where action is proposed make sure that you recap and summarise. Try to determine short-, medium- and long-term objectives, who will do things and any assistance that will be required. Be realistic.

Make sure after the meeting that you know:

- who is doing what;
- what extra resources are required before action can be taken;

- whether you need to negotiate for any resources, help, assistance;
- what are the deadlines;
- how you will know that a task is completed (completion criteria?).

It is most important that something happens and that ultimately you achieve your aim. Ensure that items in your short- and medium-term plans happen, that they are seen to heppn and that the school reviews their success.

### Activity 8 – A science co-ordinator's file
Most co-ordinators have a growing collection of documentation from school, government, course, LEAs, etc. This activity asks you to establish or review a file which you will keep. This file will allow you to have important information readily available and to show others that you are organised and that you do have your 'finger on the pulse' of the subject in school.

- What documentation do you need at hand? Add to or amend this list: school policy; action plan; monitoring plan; resources list; curriculum plan; early years; assessment; section from the school development plan; ———; ———; ———.

- Three different co-ordinators organised their files differently. Can you see advantages and disadvantages for yourself?

| Co-ordinators file A<br>File contents | Co-ordinators file B<br>File contents | Co-ordinators file C<br>File contents |
|---|---|---|
| • school documents<br>• LEAdocuments and courses<br>• government documentation | • curriculum and planning<br>• assessment<br>• INSET<br>• parents<br>• resources<br>• inspection | • action plan<br>  – teaching and learning<br>  – Science 1<br>  – monitoring<br>• resourses/IT<br>• planning<br>• assessment<br>• science policy |

- Draft out a plan for yourself and, if possible, discuss it with a collegue. Begin to construct your file. Ensure that you have it with you at meetings and courses. This file is not a school document, it is yours and so must assist you. You will soon discover items and sections you wish to add, remove or change. Keep the file itself under review. Use it to improve science in school and as concrete evidence of you as science co-ordinator actively pursuing your aims for the children's science.

Remember that you do not have to achieve everything immediately. It is more important that you have a development plan which reflects the needs of the school, has the support of the headteacher and staff and which sets out a realistic programme of activities that will lead to achieving the required goals, than that you have impressive looking documentation that will never be implemented in the classroom.

## BIBLIOGRAPHY

Harrison, M. and Cross, A. (1994) Successful curriculum change through co-ordination, in M. Harrison (ed) *Beyond the Core Curriculum*, Plymouth: Northcote House.

Cross, A. and Cross, S. (1994) Organising a professional development day, in M. Harrison (ed) *Beyond the Core Curriculum*, Plymouth: Northcote House.

Harlen, W. (1992) *The Teaching of Science*, London: David Fulton.

National Curriculum Council (1992) *Forces*, York: NCC.

National Curriculum Council (1993) *Energy*, York, NCC.

National Curriculum Council (1993) *Electricity and Magnetism*, York: NCC.

Nuffield Primary Science (1996) *Science Co-ordinators' Handbook*, London: Collins Educational.

Sherrington, R. (ed) (1993) *The ASE Primary Science Teachers Handbook*, Hemel Hempsted: ASE/Simon and Schuster.

# 14
# Monitoring and Evaluation

*Alan Cross and Alan Chin*

## INTRODUCTION

In this chapter we offer practical advice through a series of activities which will we hope further the effectiveness of the monitoring and evaluation of science in your school.

In Book 1 we gave an indication of the rationale for monitoring and evaluation. Teachers and schools have always monitored and evaluated. Developments should mean that monitoring and evaluating becomes more: **systematic**, so that it is more reliable; **broader**, so that it covers all aspects of school life; and more **useful**, so that it leads more reliably to improvement. An additional change is that the focus has moved somewhat away from the process of teaching and learning to its outcome, children's achievement. Balance between the two should be sought.

Monitoring and evaluation of curriculum areas should be part of a whole-school approach to quality control. As such it is important that the classteacher, co-ordinator and headteacher have information close at hand on which to base judgments about effectiveness. The purpose of quality control in science is to improve provision in science so that pupils' achievement is positively affected rather than be concerned about what a particular group of outsiders expect you to do.

However, with a chief inspector of schools feeling he is confident to make statements like the one below, schools need evidence to show the detail of school achievement in science and the needs of teachers and schools.

Pupils achieve well in science in a little over two-fifths of primary schools and half of secondary schools. Standards in primary school science show

194

a decline from Pre-KS1 through to KS2. Good standards are more often seen pre-KS1 and post-16. Considerable improvement is needed in KS2 in one-sixth of primary schools and in KS3 in about one-eighth of secondary schools.

He goes on to say that at Key Stage 1 'understanding of the physical sciences is weaker than that of the biological sciences because teaching tends to focus on the latter.' He says that:

Progress is more variable at Key Stage 2 with pupils making disappointing progress in around one in seven schools. The majority of pupils do gain a broader, deeper and more structured view of science and by the end of the Key Stage, are beginning to handle some more abstract scientific ideas.

(Woodhead, 1996, p. 21)

Very few of those involved in primary education would say that there is no scope for improvement. Such scope appears to revolve around the related questions of **what science is taught** and **how is science taught and learned**? However, it is the **achievement of pupils in science** which must lead you to those questions. It may be tempting simply to address the questions and in doing so at least feel that you are active. It is our belief that as your time is very precious, you should focus your activity as much as possible. It is worth adding that rarely is one source of evidence sufficient. Teachers and schools require a breadth of information to consider alongside test scores which may have a limited contribution on their own.

At this stage it may be useful to re-read the introduction to this section in Book 1 (Bk. 1, Cross and Chin, 14) where we spoke of the reasons why schools need to monitor and evaluate science in primary schools. The key points were that we are accountable and schools need to be systematic and thorough. We must know what pupils are achieving in science. We should consider all relevant aspects of the school which impinge on, in this case, science. Where there appears to be a problem or a question we should know the cause or be actively seeking it. Most importantly, once a cause is determined we must act to resolve the situation.

In Book 1 we defined monitoring as 'determination of the extent to which agreed plans are being implemented' and evaluation as 'the process by which these plans and their implementation are judged to have achieved what they set out to achieve' (Russell, 1994).

We emphasised the need for senior management to provide

195

resources, mainly in terms of time. This point must be re-emphasised. Full-time classteachers will be unable to devote more than a few hours a term to monitoring and evaluation of science. Thus classteachers should have time for straightforward evaluation of their classes' achievement and their own lessons. To ask them to do much more than this is perhaps asking too much. For the science co-ordinator the situation is even more challenging, as they seek quite detailed information about achievement and teaching. Concrete efforts should therefore be made by the senior management of a school to say, yes we want monitoring and evaluation in science and this is how we will ensure that it occurs.

When planning these activities we had in mind the model for developing and implementing a monitoring and evaluation plan which we presented in Book 1. We have divided our activities into four broad areas: first, reassuring colleagues about the process; second, establishing the picture in your school; third, clarifying a view of your expectations; and last, establishing a pattern or system of monitoring and evaluation.

## PART ONE – ESTABLISHING A PICTURE OF PRESENT PRACTICE

### Activity 1 – Looking at the science picture in the whole school

(Time required: 2 hours)

Here we ask that whether your focus is your classroom or the whole school, you look carefully at the science that is going on. Beware of one-line answers to these questions – you will be **describing a range of practice**. Your answers should reflect the full range of what is going on. You want to know:

- about levels of achievement in science;

- about science planning across the school;

- how much science is occurring;

- how often science goes on;

- when and where science occurs;

- how science is taught;

- the amount of practical work;

- whether children carry out investigations;
- about resources available.

We have provided a proforma for such an audit in Figure 14.1. You might take a general look or focus on particular items in turn. It is likely that you will find areas as you go along which require a little more scrutiny. Remember at this stage you are interested in finding out what is happening (monitoring); don't be too concerned about making judgments (evaluating). You should inform the headteacher about what you are doing. At this stage you are unlikely to have access to other classrooms. Advice is given later about doing this.

---

### Initial Science Audit (Classroom/School)

*Amount of science?*
Time allocation?
Length of sessions?
When does science occur?

*Documentation*
Do you have a policy, a
scheme, a curriculum plan?
What planning formats are
used?

*Nature of science?*
How is science taught?
By whom is science taught?
How much practical work?
Emphasis on Sc. 1?

*Evidence of achievement*
Any science records?
Scores from testing?
Teacher assessment results?

*INSET*
Activities?
Needs?

*Children's achievement*
Is achievement in line
with expectations?
Are there individuals or
groups who lie outside
those expectations?

*Special Educational Needs*

*Equal opportunities*

*Resources*
What resources are used?
How easily available are
those resources?
Information re spending?

*Safety*

*Other issues?*

---

Fig. 14.1. Initial science audit

## Activity 2 – What have I learnt?

(Time required: 1 hour)

You now need to look at the evidence you have gathered, to determine what it is telling you and where you need more information. Make a copy of the blank proforma used in Activity 1. This time label it 'where we are' and make a summary on it of where the school/classroom appears to be.

## Activity 3 – Taking stock/reporting the situation

(Time required: 1 hour)

Review the above so that you can analyse the evidence collected and identify areas of concern. We would suggest that you use this activity to prepare a short statement summarising the position to your headteacher and ideally colleagues (discuss this with your head-teacher).

- Can you summarise progress to date?

- Can you summarise the point which science has reached in your school?

- Can you summarise the achievement of the children?

- Have strengths appeared?

- Are there areas of concern?

- Do you have thoughts about possible future steps?

## Activity 4 – Monitoring and evaluation as a whole-school issue

(Time required: 1–2 hours)

This may be the right time to discuss the monitoring and evaluation of science with a member of the school's senior management team. In most cases this will mean some discussion with the head. In some schools a deputy or senior teacher will be involved.

Prior to such discussion determine:

- Are the aims of science clear to you?

- What do you mean by monitoring and evaluating science?

- Have you collected together all the evidence available?

Have you conducted some analysis of the present situation (see Activity 3)?

- What are you proposing to the headteacher?

What are you proposing?

- That science be monitored and evaluated?

- That science be more systematically monitored and evaluated?

- That the place of science in the school development plan be reviewed?

- That policy be reviewed to reflect developments in practice?

- That particular access be negotiated? For you to visit classrooms? For you to see teachers' planning?

- That the issue may be discussed with other staff? Senior management? Whole staff?

- That you be given time to:
  – meet the assessment co-ordinator?
  – visit classrooms?
  – provide for training of colleagues or yourself?

- That you construct a plan of action re monitoring and evaluating in science?

## PART TWO – CLARIFYING EXPECTATIONS

### Activity 5 – Expectations
(Time required: 1 hour)
You and your colleagues need to be able to form judgments about achievement. In order to do this you need to have realistic and yet demanding expectations of your children. If you base your judgments solely on experience of teaching one age range for a year or two in one school there is a good chance that you will be wide of the mark. It will benefit you if you are a science co-ordinator to extend this activity by visiting other primary schools and perhaps seeing work that goes on at Key Stage 3.

This activity can be conducted by one teacher or a group or whole staff. The more people involved the wider the effect within a school. It is in some ways similar to school moderation exercises. You might like to use Figure 14.2.

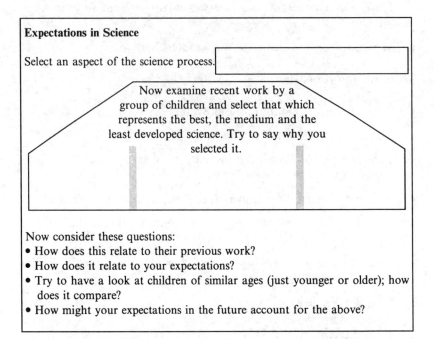

**Expectations in Science**

Select an aspect of the science process.

Now examine recent work by a group of children and select that which represents the best, the medium and the least developed science. Try to say why you selected it.

Now consider these questions:
• How does this relate to their previous work?
• How does it relate to your expectations?
• Try to have a look at children of similar ages (just younger or older); how does it compare?
• How might your expectations in the future account for the above?

Fig. 14.2. Reviewing expectations in science

### Activity 6 – Three tray exercise
(Time required: 1–2 hours)
(See Figure 14.3.) This is a further attempt to moderate expectations. The classteacher designates the work of three children who in the teacher's opinion provide an example of: below average attainment of the class, average attainment of the class and above average attainment of the class. The co-ordinator then looks at and comments on the work selected. Comments are made by the co-ordinator to the classteacher who might later seek clarification. Thus the co-ordinator has the opportunity to examine work from every class.

### Activity 7 – Visiting other classes
(Time required: 2 hour+)
In Book 1 we emphasised the need for senior management to provide resources, mainly in terms of time. At some point we would say that every co-ordinator needs to spend time in the classes of other teachers and with other age ranges.

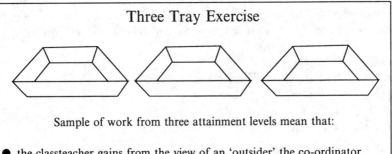

Fig. 14.3. Three tray exercise

This is one of the most expensive forms of monitoring and evaluation, but it is also the one with the most potential. Teacher colleagues need to be reassured about any visit you might be making to their classroom. What is this visit for? What will be the results? Who will see the results? What will happen during the visit? The potential and ideas for such meetings are discussed in Book 1 and ought at this stage to be reviewed.

The question of anonymity is important to deal with. We would suggest that the co-ordinator does not make direct reports to the head about members of staff except in serious cases; for example, a safety issue. In all cases where problems arise it would be most appropriate for the teacher to see the head. The co-ordinator ought to provide the head with a general summary, without identifying staff, of issues which face the school.

It might be a good idea to save this option until you have gathered as much other information as possible. When you have completed Activity 3 you may be in a better position to determine the focus of classroom visits. It may be a good idea to have a whole-school focus, e.g. Science 1, teachers' questions, children's response, and add one or two issues from each individual teacher. It might be easier to negotiate time to do this if you aim to visit all classes on a two-year rolling programme. Such visits are very useful prior to inspection by outsiders as they get everyone more used to the notion of 'outsiders' visiting classrooms.

It is therefore important for the science co-ordinator and teacher to meet prior to the session to look at termly and weekly plans and to agree what will happen during the visit. It is essential to have a meeting afterwards to agree **what did happen** and **where you will go next.**

*Before the visit agree*:

- what is the purpose of the visit;

- the time of the visit;

- the focus of the visit;

- the co-ordinator's role (see Book 1 for a range of options);

- the classteacher's role;

- in what form the outcomes will be, e.g. children's work, a tape recording, written notes;

- the time for and duration of feedback and discussion;

- that the results of this visit will not be seen by **anyone** else.

*During the visit ensure that*:

- plans are kept to;

- the children's achievement in science is the focus;

- you examine work from a range of children;

- you acknowledge problems which the teacher may be facing;

- you make notes.

*After the visit ensure that*:

- you hold the feedback session;

- you keep to the time agreed;

- you start by asking the teacher's view on the focus and out-come;

- you seek to agree on good aspects of the session as well as areas which might need attention;

- you come to an agreement about the outcome and the action which might be taken (if this is to involve another member of staff, the teacher must agree).

Figure 14.4 gives some sample proformas for classroom visits.

**Planning a Co-ordinator's Visit to a Classroom**

Class

Teacher

Year

Date

Focus of visit

Whole-school focus

Class focus

Science to be observed

Classteacher's role

Co-ordinator's role

Date and time of follow up meeting

Please initial..............
..............

copy to co-ordinator, copy to classteacher

**Follow Up to Classroom Visit**
Please refer to planning sheet.
Date of meeting.........

Agreed outcomes

Children's achievement

Teaching

| Action | By whom | By when | To be reviewed |
|--------|---------|---------|----------------|
|        |         |         |                |

Please initial ..............
..............

copy to co-ordinator, copy to classteacher

Fig. 14.4. Proformas for planning and reviewing visits to classrooms

## PART THREE – ESTABLISHING PATTERNS AND SYSTEMS FOR MONITORING AND EVALUATION IN SCIENCE

In Part Three we look to permanent systems which can ensure that monitoring and evaluation of science continues. The approach of 'who? what? how? and when?' which was exemplified in Book 1 is now offered as a useful framework for seeing how a number of professionals in school can contribute. We then suggest a format for an annual review, and plan in the short and medium term a three-year rolling cycle which aims to produce development in the teaching and learning of science.

### Activity 8 – Who? what? how? and when?
(Time required: 1 hour)

If you have completed the activities to this point you will have already tackled a range of tasks and will have gathered a range of information about your school's science. Some strategies will have worked better than others. We suggest that you look back at Chapter 14 in Book 1 and the example of Light Oaks Junior School. Can you map out your proposed approach to monitoring and evaluation on the proforma in Figure 14.5?

| Name of School: Monitoring and Evaluation of Science | | | |
|---|---|---|---|
| **Who?** | **What?** | **How?** | **When?** |
| Class teachers | | | |
| Co-ordinator | | | |
| Senior management team | | | |

Fig. 14.5. Proforma to summarise monitoring and evaluation procedures

---

**Development Plan Review**

**Review of Previous Academic Year 1999_ – 199_**

Children's achievement

KS1

KS2

Curriculum

Staff

Resources

---

Fig. 14.6. Development plan review of previous year

## Activity 9 – Reflecting monitoring and evaluation in your long- and medium-term plans

(Time required: 2 hours)

Here we provide a framework for you to make a review of achievement to date and to set goals in the medium and long term. (See Figure 14.6.)

In each case a summary is required. Under 'children's achievement' we suggest that you refer to Key Stages 1 and 2 separately, while nevertheless ensuring that you avoid treating them as two quite separate entities. You are not referring to evidence here (of course, you should have some available to back up your claims); rather you are identifying general trends. Beware of attempting to reduce everything to a few words – don't lose the detail. Beware of using too many words. On the occasions that this document is read by someone else we suggest that you are on hand to interpret it.

The second section which refers to the curriculum ought to focus on the teaching and learning of both process (Science 1) and content.

Has there been balance? Have there been initiatives? How does the school's overall curricular planning affect science? Is there time for science?

The section on staff should give a summary, identify areas of strength and weaker areas, note INSET, responsibilities, involvement of outside agencies.

Finally consider resource strengths and weaknesses, include teaching areas, teaching resources, teacher resources, the school site and resources further afield. Always be clear about what is needed and exactly how it will improve achievement. The two forecast plans referring to this coming year and years to follow (Figures 14.7 and 14.8) ought, if used carefully and updated each year, to provide you with significant direction.

Such plans would help to give coherence to a science co-ordinator's file as mentioned in the previous chapter.

---

**Science Development Plan   199_ – 199_**

**Children's achievement**

KS1


KS2


Curriculum


Staff


Resources

---

Fig. 14.7. Development plan for the current academic year

| Science Development Plan |
|---|
| **Projected Plan for 199_ – 199_** |
| Children's achievement |
| KS1 |
| KS2 |
| Curriculum |
| Staff |
| Resources |

Fig. 14.8. Science development plan – projection

## CONCLUSION

This section may be the most important part of this book for senior managers and science co-ordinators. Resources, both financial and professional, are limited. If monitoring and evaluation are thorough and aimed at raising achievement in young children, they provide a powerful management tool. Professionals can be confident in the decisions they make and use limited resources to good effect.

## BIBLIOGRAPHY

Russell, S. (1994) *Ready for Action: a Practical Guide to Post-Ofsted Action Planning*, Leamington Spa: Courseware Publications.
Woodhead, C. (1996) *The Annual Report of Her Majesty's Chief Inspector: 1996*, London: HMSO.

# Index

art, 91
audit, 76, 132, 174, 197
anti-racist, 68
assessment. 21, 29, 98, 102, 112, 189, 197–9
  and record keeping, 128
  formative, 52, 120, 127
  teaching learning and assessment, 76, 115, 116–22, 192
  self assessment, 112, 116, 122
  statutory, 127
  summative, 114, 127–8
attainment, 200
attainment targets, 98, 114
AT1, 97–115
attitudes, 70

class, 59, 64, 72
classrooms, 36, 50, 97–8, 188, 196–203
  management, 125, 128, 144, 190
  organisation, 37, 71
  strategies, 59, 89, 106, 117
  resources, 132
concepts, 8–10, 31, 39
  maps, 16, 52, 116, 124–5
  development, 30, 44–8, 93, 95
  scientific, 21, 75, 86, 98
constructivism, 21, 116–7
communication, 111
computers, 136–7, 144, 151, 189
co-ordinator, 59, 101, 133, 137, 176, 192–3, 194–207
culture, 71–3, 178–81

curriculum, 33, 34, 70, 101, 106, 114, 150, 154, 168, 194, 205
cross-curricular, 137, 154, 156, 160, 162

differentiation, 34–7, 54–7, 102, 107
  task, 55
  outcome, 55
discussion, 12, 24–6, 32, 49–50, 53, 63–7, 106, 113, 118, 139, 155, 169–70, 173–4, 186–91, 198
drawings, 11, 16

early years, 75, 79, 81, 89, 95, 130, 192
English, 72, 156
environment, 9, 140
  learning, 95
  social, 70
equality, 59, 70, 71–2, 173
equal opportunities, 64, 197
equipment, 90, 132
evaluation, 127, 137, 142, 178, 187, 194–207
experiment, 15, 17, 23, 29, 98, 106, 117, 137, 185

fair testing, 40, 80, 101–6, 146
food, 80
forces, 16, 77, 179, 185

gender, 59, 64, 72
group work, 16, 37–42, 50, 52, 63, 89, 94, 112, 117, 128